10-10-12

to RYAN - a
good guy FROM a
good FAMILY.

Larry

CALL
OF THE
COUCH

A FAMILY'S LOVE AFFAIR WITH ITS BUSINESS, SCHNEIDERMAN'S FURNITURE

LARRY SCHNEIDERMAN
with Jody Mabry

BEAVER'S
POND
PRESS

With Jody Mabry

ISBN 13: 978-1-59298-925-6

Library of Congress Catalog Number: 2014940873

Printed in the United States of America

First Printing: 2014

18 17 16 15 14   5 4 3 2 1

Cover and interior design by James Monroe Design, LLC.

BEAVER'S
POND
PRESS

Beaver's Pond Press, Inc.
7108 Ohms Lane
Edina, MN 55439–2129
(952) 829–8818
www.BeaversPondPress.com

To order, visit www.LarrySchneiderman.com
or www.BeaversPondBooks.com
or call (800) 901-3480. Reseller discounts available.

To Sheila

From the very first moment I saw you
That's when I knew
All the dreams I held in my heart
Had suddenly come true.

—David Gray, "Be Mine"

CONTENTS

PREFACE

I am Larry Schneiderman of Schneiderman's Furniture. In 1948, my parents, Max and Edna Schneiderman, bought a small, broken-down general store in the rural township of Elmer, Minnesota, about 45 miles northwest of Duluth, in an area of the state known as the Iron Range. I'm one of six children. Oldest to youngest, we are David, Karen, Phillip, Claudia, Larry, and Russell. I worked in the family store growing up, as did most of my brothers and sisters. From the humble beginnings of an ill-stocked general store, Schneiderman's Furniture has grown to include six large stores in the Minnesota cities of Duluth, Lakeville, Roseville, Woodbury, Plymouth, and Rochester.

As I write this, I am 64 years old. I feel fortunate to be celebrating my 43rd year of marriage with my wife, Sheila, and am blessed with three great children, Jason, Jodi, and Jenna. Together we form a strong and supportive family.

When I get together with friends, businesspeople, neighbors, and virtually anybody else, the inevitable question pops up, "When are you going to retire?" I don't find the question offensive or invasive, but I have no immediate plans to retire. If the conversation continues, often the topic moves on to Social Security, pensions, and—God help me—Medicare and health insurance. Soon, the question morphs into, "Why *don't* you want to retire?"

The fact is, I still love the furniture business! I sold my first piece of furniture in my parents' store when I was 15 years old and I've been hooked ever since. Of course, sooner or later, everyone's career comes to an end and mine will too. But in the meantime, I get so much meaning and enjoyment from working with the people at our company, the people we buy from, and the people who make it all happen—our customers. I am honored to work with my son, Jason, who loves the business as much as I do. I've rarely suffered a bad day at work. I like to get there early, and when I'm driving home, I think back about the day with satisfaction. It's been extremely gratifying and, like my parents before me, I have no regrets whatsoever that Schneiderman's Furniture has been my life's work.

I may have gotten involved in the furniture business to please my parents. I am a "people pleaser" at heart, and it felt good to have my parents appreciate what I was doing to help them grow the business. When I look back at those early years, it's clear that we were all learning the business together as a family. Each person in the family played a role in our ultimate success story. While I didn't consciously think about it at the time, I was learning so many life lessons beyond the furniture business. From Mom and Dad, I learned the importance of hard work, teamwork, problem solving, time management, friendship, resilience, loyalty, and most of all, the joy of loving your work.

Being successful at starting and nurturing a business into a flourishing concern is something most people never experience. From an early age, the business looked challenging, financially rewarding, and fun! But there was more. It became apparent that making customers happy made me happy.

This book really started on my 60th birthday, surrounded by about a dozen friends and family members as we enjoyed a nice dinner at Porterhouse, one of my favorite local restaurants—though I am always disappointed by the lack of a wedge salad on their menu. It's a steakhouse, after all! I was seated next to my daughter, Jodi. She and I began to laugh over the notion of "bucket lists." She asked what's on mine. I confessed four things—and the third was writing a book to get my parents' story on paper so they'll be remembered for what they achieved. "There are so many stories you haven't heard about your grandparents and how they started the business," I told her.

As I began to think about how to tell the whole tale—which seemed overwhelming at times—I began to remember more stories and anecdotes I hadn't recalled for years. Some of them feature my dad's occasionally "salty" expressions. After all, he served in the Navy and worked twenty years in a steel mill. Though his earthy view of life may offend some, I chose not to alter the stories. I want this book to be as accurate a reflection of our family story as possible. As I worked to capture my own recollections, gather what memories my siblings were willing to share, and glimpse the past through my mom's journals, my respect for my parents grew. I made exciting new discoveries and made connections only possible with the passage of decades.

At times during the process of writing this book, I definitely wondered why I tackled it. The process has proven far more difficult than I imagined at the outset. I always knew I would have to finish, though. I'm an avid reader and I've never started a book without finishing. That's the kind of closure junky I am.

As I progressed, my initial goal of a story for my family morphed into something larger. I shared what I had written with a couple of close business friends who encouraged me to continue—and convinced me that a broader audience might be interested in this story. As a life-long participant in building a company, I have witnessed and been a part of encountering, managing, and solving a long list of challenges. I hope some of the reflections and anecdotes included in this book will be useful to other businesspeople—even Schneiderman's employees.

While each business has its particular set of circumstances, many challenges are recognizable to all of us. Perhaps Schneiderman's nearly 70 years of learning as we go will help another business steer around some obstacles and stay true to its core ideals. I hope so.

In some ways, the furniture business mirrors the apparel business. There are new and exciting styles, colors, and fabrics constantly being offered. It's fun to buy and to sell the ever-shifting wardrobe of furniture. It's a real high to help people find what they need or what looks best in their homes. Magic words from the customer such as, "Let's go ahead with this," sound very sweet indeed! My hope is that every time a customer buys from one of our stores, we have created a customer for life.

On occasion friends have asked if I ever considered doing something different. The plain truth is that I did not. It strikes me as strange to admit it, but I'm certain that had I been asked at 16 if I would still be selling furniture almost 50 years later, I very likely would have said, "Absolutely!"

I wrote this book to share my family's genuine, made-in-America narrative of how two people who started with no financial resources achieved great success through their hard work and determination. My family, like our country, has seen good times and tough times. Difficulties come and they go—but successful people push on regardless. They work together to envision and then accomplish goals. Successful people don't dwell on mistakes; instead, they learn from them. They make the right choices in the present while shaping a plan for the future. I have experienced an American success story firsthand and it is my privilege to share it with you.

P.S. What else was on the bucket list I confessed to Jodi at the birthday dinner? Well, number one was a trip to South Africa. Done. Number two, a trip tracing the Apostle Paul's journey in Greece and Turkey. That file's still open. You're reading the third item on my list right now. (Whew!) And, when Jodi pressed me about number four, I replied, "Here I am, 60 years old, and I've never smoked pot." I learned something else from my parents: It's good to keep your kids guessing.

INTRODUCTION

Ask any attorney and they'll tell you that businesspeople in general and entrepreneurs in particular make poor trial witnesses. Why? We come to believe our experiences represent widespread, even universal, truths.

As far back as the height of ancient Greece and Rome, it was common for successful people to write maxims, statements they viewed as fundamental principles of their success. Consider, for example, one of Thomas Jefferson's pithy sayings: "Never buy what you do not want because it is cheap; it will be dear to you." (In addition to their universal implications, those words of caution are also good advice in the furniture business.)

My father's approach to the challenges of life and business tended to be quite polarized. For him, an issue was rarely colored in shades of gray. Dad proclaimed his success was based on a three-legged stool of unwavering principles: Don't waste money on advertising. Don't have sales. Don't use commissions. Well, those beliefs worked for him, but it wasn't long before the growth of the company required doing the absolute opposite.

My business "truths" aren't fixed rules. They are also not presented as a manual for how to run your company. Good business books filled with essential knowledge abound and they shouldn't be ignored. The discoveries I've made emerged anecdotally—in unexpected moments and often from unanticipated sources—and you'll find them presented in much the same way throughout these pages. My lessons are woven into my family's story of transforming the small, rundown general store my parents purchased in a rural township in northern Minnesota into a solid company with multiple locations in the Twin Cities metro area and Duluth. Many of my most cherished discoveries and beliefs are backed by my faith. Others I learned and adopted through years of collaboration with my family, employees, customers, and friends.

Maxims and storytelling are two ways we share experiences from generation to generation, and sometimes from era to era. This book represents my entry in that long tradition.

Below are a few of the central truths I've discovered—my Minnesota maxims, so to speak. They serve as a preview of what you'll read in the coming chapters. I am highlighting them because, though they have been pivotal to my success, I haven't found them articulated in quite the same way elsewhere.

Find a way to not say no to our customers and our associates. You'll notice I didn't put this in the traditional, positive spin—find a way to say yes. Saying yes as often as you can is a slam dunk, especially in retail. I'm talking about those situations in which saying no is the simplest and most tempting path, instead of seeking out a middle ground where at least something can be offered. I've been around far too many conversations in which businesspeople rant about how crazy some customers can be. There's even a website devoted to allowing these unhappy people to vent. Experience has shown me that in almost any situation, you can offer up something that demonstrates your appreciation of the customer. I feel the same about working with our associates. HR policies need to be enforced consistently, but often with some creativity and extra effort, we can find a way to help. In cases of potential conflict with customers and employees, figuring out how to avoid saying no leads to stronger relationships and healthy compromise that leaves everyone feeling more satisfied. "No" is often the easy, and ultimately less useful, way out of a problem.

Reputation is everything. My dad's three "never" rules were anchored with his conviction to never spend money on advertising. He didn't need to—in those days our satisfied customers were our marketing. Even though today we spend a significant amount on traditional marketing and advertising, I still believe the most important tool for growing our sales remains word of mouth. It remains a tangible factor in our success, and it can't be bought and paid for. Good word of mouth validates our ongoing efforts to serve our customers well—and that's why we're here.

Sometimes letting an employee go is better all around. Schneiderman's is a slow-to-react company when it comes time to let somebody go. I'm not proud of that, but it's deep into our culture to help all our employees succeed. Sometimes I've literally had to step in and take action because a clearly necessary firing just wasn't happening. A smart business consultant once told me he could tell if a company isn't doing well in this area by asking, "When an employee leaves, do you or any of your managers ever say, 'It's a good thing so-and-so is leaving'?" Healthy companies take action when necessary. They don't wait for a failing employee to make the decision about whether to stay or go.

Do all you can to improve your odds of hiring the right people for the job. Business owners and managers sometimes believe they've been given some special gift of intuition when it comes to hiring people. I admit to giving myself too much credit on that front long ago. Several bad choices are all it takes to realize we need to do all we can to improve our odds. It's a mistake to take shortcuts in hiring. I remind myself often that for our customers, Schneiderman's is whomever we put in front of them. Even with policies that require two separate interviews, several tests, and calling references, I still think it's a crapshoot. The odds definitely improve, though, by taking these steps. If I have to gamble, I want to improve the odds so we have our best chance to make each customer's experience with us a good one.

Success requires managers who exhibit the company's values. We've built our policies around the proven fact that the way employees view their manager parallels the way they view the company. So if an employee thinks her manager is committed to the mission of Schneiderman's and is fair, she likely believes the company is committed to its stated mission and operates in a fair manner. If, on the other hand, the employee thinks the manager doesn't care, he likely thinks the company doesn't care.

In retail, avoid people who can't project a positive, happy attitude. Some people like to announce as if it's a badge of honor, "I'm not a morning person." We all know what that means. Of course, everyone has their off days, but all in all, I really think it's our responsibility, if not our mission, to make the day just a little bit better for those we encounter. I mean, if we look like we don't want to be there, why would our customers feel differently? It may sound naïve, but I buy into the saying, "If you act enthusiastic, you'll be enthusiastic."

The importance of momentum can't be overstated. Unfortunately, I've witnessed the marriages of several friends end in divorce over the years. In each case, the signs were there. Little problems became big problems as they spiraled downward. If you believe relationships are important in business—as I do—it won't be a stretch to recognize that some of the same challenges exist in business relationships as in a marriage. When challenging events strain your mutual respect, one of you has to take the initiative to reverse the trend before the relationship becomes damaged beyond repair. That's true of relationships in general. Similarly, when a business relationship is going well, the momentum encourages good things to continue building. This is often the best time to take bold initiatives.

This notion of momentum applies not only to relationships, but to the business as a whole. Time and again, I've noticed when sales are on the rise, we gain traction to build further on the trending. Sometimes it's tempting to sit back and feel satisfied, but a better strategy is to consider innovative new choices. Of course, the same principle applies when momentum is moving downward. It can seem as if suddenly all sorts of new problems crop up. It's likely the situation will continue to feel somewhat embattled until the momentum is turned around.

Always find the root cause of the problem before you start treating its symptoms. I'm consistently amazed at how often even experienced and competent associates treat the symptoms instead of the causes of a problem with a customer. Most of our managers know the first thing I'm going to ask them when they have a challenge is what caused the problem. Only by locating the issue that initiated the problem can we find an effective way to respond.

Keep asking: "How will this affect our customers?" It's vital in a retail setting to keep the customer experience at the forefront of our ongoing decision-making. It comes as a pleasant surprise to me how often one of our associates will ask that fundamental question and reverse course because the answer was "not in a good way." In those moments they are representing our company's core values. Similarly, decisions that have a detrimental effect on employees cost a company just as dearly since employees inevitably reflect their negative feelings to customers.

Like my father's bold statement about the three legs of his success, perhaps my list of key business truths will be refuted by future experiences—but I seriously doubt it. (I imagine my father would have said the same!) I guess we'll have to check back with my son, Jason, in 30 years to find out.

1

A Small Store's Haunted Beginnings

Schneiderman's Furniture began in a small country store. But before I get too far into the story of my family's business, it's important to set the scene—to tell how small-town politics and a violent end led to Schneiderman's beginnings. My family wasn't directly involved. In fact, we're an afterthought in this violent episode of the small township of Elmer, Minnesota, and an even smaller little store.

Joe Constanzi, an Italian immigrant, didn't build the two-story grocery store in Elmer township, but he certainly made something of it, and not by selling groceries. In fact, as I understand it, he didn't carry enough inventory to make a business out of groceries. Which is probably why he applied for a liquor license—or as it's called in municipal documents archived in Elmer, an off-sale beer license—in January 1948.

Joe was 33 years old then, with a wife and a six-year-old daughter. Like many people—including my dad Max Schneiderman—Joe's dream was owning a store. Running a store in

Elmer at that time must have been difficult, since the area is not only rural, it's remote. Elmer township is four miles from the small town of Meadowlands, and sits northwest of Duluth, Minnesota, a prosperous port city built on the shipping industry through the Great Lakes. Elmer was a small community hidden amidst swamp, prairie, and farmland. Even the thriving lumber and iron industries seemed to skip over the area.

In order to succeed, or likely just to make ends meet, Joe would have needed an off-sale beer license. He had applied to the town board several times before, and each application was denied. According to the records, the board's reasoning was that Elmer was too small to have more than one off-sale beer license. The only establishment in the township that had one was the Old Oaken Bucket, owned by Albert Bernsdorf, a voting member of the town board. You can probably imagine why Joe was frustrated.

In the weeks leading up to the board meeting on January 31, when his latest application was to be considered, Joe had been more vocal about the discrimination he felt was building up against him. While he may not have been able to prove the reason for the discrimination, he had a good idea it was due to him being the competition in a small town. Joe had only lived in Elmer for two years. Though he had secured contracts—both handshake and formal—to provide hot lunches to the school, and a variety of other town agreements, he felt there was pressure to put him out of business.

Joe's first public grievance was lodged against the school board when Frank Svoboda, the township clerk and the school bus driver, willfully failed to stop the school bus in front of Constanzi's store for the "kiddies to buy candy." Their handshake agreement to do so, while acknowledged by the board, was dismissed because it wasn't formally declared. A week after the first petition, Joe filed a second formal complaint when the Elmer Community Club, while under contract with him, decided to purchase meals from another grocery store in nearby Meadowlands.

In light of these recent incidents and his record of previous denials for an off-sale beer license, Joe was determined to attend the town board meeting on January 31. On that Saturday, snow covered the ground outside the Elmer schoolhouse where the town board met. Despite one of the worst winters in recorded history, that afternoon the 23-degree temperature was a reprieve from frequent sub-zero days. The small two-story schoolhouse resembled thousands of similar buildings in use throughout the United States during the 1940s. The first floor was a large room with folding doors that could separate it into two teaching areas. At times—for Christmas plays and community events—the doors would fold open to create a single large room. Each end of the schoolhouse had an entry that could be used when the rooms were separated. Likewise, a staircase was located at each end of the schoolhouse leading to the teacherage upstairs. The teacherage had two bedrooms (one for each teacher), one bathroom, one kitchen, and a living area. Behind the schoolhouse was a back door that led to the water pump and janitorial supplies. The town board, and later, Joe Constanzi, entered the building through the back door.

As his wife later reported, Joe stormed out of his small country store on his way to the meeting. He slammed the door as he left, muttering something about "taking care" of the town board. In one hand, he carried a .30-30 caliber rifle and in his other, a pistol. He already had a suspicion about how the vote would go. Surely Joe's wife was concerned as he left, but it's difficult to believe she could have imagined the day would end as it did.

Joe stepped out of his truck at 4:35 p.m. He was angry, and likely nervous. I can picture his anxiety growing and his fists clenching as he walked past the cars belonging to the town board members who would soon be voting on his appeal for an off-sale license. Albert Dupac, Emil Makela, and Alois Ringhofer, all members of the town board, along with Frank Svoboda (township clerk), and Albert Bernsdorf (treasurer), were already gathered for the formal meeting of the board.

When Joe walked up to the schoolhouse, he didn't carry the guns he'd walked out of his store holding. As angry and focused on the upcoming meeting as he likely was, he probably didn't notice the small snow fort some schoolchildren had built into a snowbank behind the school.

After Joe stepped inside the building, he had to wait for them to make a decision on his beer license. There was no doubt Joe was concerned. He'd already devised a plan if the town board denied him the license.

Joe stood as the board members unanimously rejected his application as their first order of business. "Is that your final word?" he demanded.

"It is," Svoboda said, as he began to sign the rejection.

Constanzi dashed from the schoolhouse, muttering, "You'll be sorry."

The board had already begun to discuss their next agenda item as Joe seized the .30–30 caliber rifle from his truck. In less than a minute, he walked back into the schoolhouse, entered the room, and began shooting. It was now around 4:45.

Svoboda, his pen still in hand, was the first hit. He staggered a few steps toward Joe and then fell. Constanzi then turned the rifle on Dupac, who after a shot to the chest fell dead between two rows of desks. Makela, the board president, tried to escape through the front doors, but couldn't open them, so he ran upstairs to the teacherage. One shot cut through his stomach as he climbed the stairs. Ringhofer was hit by one of the bullets in the arm as he tried to follow Makela up the stairs to the teacherage. He later commented that he should have known the front doors were locked, but in the confusion, he forgot. Makela died while standing, and then collapsed. Ringhofer then ran back down the stairs, managed to unlock the front doors, and escaped. From there he ran across the field to his home, trailing blood as he ran.

Albert Bernsdorf, the holder of the township's only off-sale beer permit, escaped unscathed, except for a big toe, which he broke while running out of the building. He hid in the snow fort built by the schoolchildren. He said he heard a few more shots and then a lot of banging, as if Constanzi were trying to break open a door with the butt-end of his gun. It was at this time he must have shot Emil Makela one more time.

Joe lingered for a few moments in the room where the children of his victims attended school. Desks, windows, and the blackboard were marred by flying bullets. Sheriff Owens later determined that at least a dozen shots were fired.

By the time Constanzi made his getaway in his truck, the alarm had been spread. Armed farmers volunteered to help Sheriff Owens in the search.

Shortly after the sheriff arrived on the scene, Constanzi's truck was found about a mile from the schoolhouse, near the home of Hjalmer Carlson, a self-employed lumberjack. The impromptu posse cautiously surrounded Hjalmer's shack. When they closed in through the heavy snow, they found Constanzi's body about fifty feet from the hut. He had shot himself through the head.

Before Constanzi took his life, he chatted nervously with Hjalmer Carlson. Carlson, describing the conversation, said Constanzi admitted the shooting to him and said he had prepared a letter for Sheriff Owens. "I told him to go home to his wife and kids," Carlson told officials afterwards, "but he just told me to be sure to give Sheriff Owens the letter and he wouldn't be around much longer."

Carlson said Constanzi then emptied his pockets on the table. He took out a penknife and 56 cents. "Give the money to my little girl," Constanzi told Carlson.

"He promised not to hurt me and then he left," Carlson said. "Next thing I knew, the sheriff's deputies had surrounded my place and told me Constanzi was dead."

Constanzi's farewell note charged board members with discrimination in handling beer permit licenses. He contended he had just as much right to sell beer as Albert Bernsdorf. Constanzi charged that while the board was discriminating against him, it was permitting 16-year-old children into the tavern, the Old Oaken Bucket, in violation of state laws.

After a cryptic farewell to his family, he ended his note with a postscript: "And if the newspapers get this, be sure they get the facts about the liquor license straight."

Less than four hours after the killings, Sheriff Owens marked the case closed. Joe Constanzi was buried in nearby Hibbing, Minnesota; those he killed are buried closer to Elmer.

I remember being curious about the incident when I was growing up. As the years pass and the immediacy of incidents like this fades, we slowly forget their significance. The event is rarely mentioned anymore, but at the time it was captured in newspaper clippings from around the country. The story was even covered in *Life* magazine. Descendants of the men Joe Constanzi killed still live in and around Elmer today. The subject of the shooting rarely comes up as a reminder that this rural and isolated community had its own mass murder. Though the incident is in the distant past now, buildings and memories still stand as a reminder of how that event in 1948 affected so many lives, even to this day.

It was shortly after the shooting that my parents purchased Elmer's small grocery store from Signe Constanzi, Joe's widow.

As Frank Sramek, a friend and long-time Elmer resident puts it, "Only a short time transpired and the store was sold. Max and Edna Schneiderman seemed to appear out of nowhere, is the best way I can describe it."

2

Max and Edna, the Early Years

Every time someone dies unexpectedly, we're impressed with the fact that we're expendable—and have you noticed, usually the remarks are, "How sad to die before a ripe old age," unless the person is aged?

I remember very well my tears at my father's funeral. They were tears of regret that he had been cheated out of living a full life. If I had read some memoirs written by him in his early, vital years I might not have felt so bitter. So, [I write this] just so no one will say, "Poor Eddie—she was so tied down with the store, and children, and really didn't have a chance to do all the things she'd have liked doing."

These are the words of my mother, Edna Kretzschmar Schneiderman, written in July 1957. She was born on December 12, 1912, and she passed away on November 12, 2013, at 100 years of age, almost 101. While the troubles of aging had begun to creep up on her, until the end she was still poignantly faithful to her family and God—two things she cherished more in life than anything else.

Edna "Eddie" Kretzschmar's father, Martin, was a Missouri Synod Lutheran pastor who suffered from epilepsy, was confined to state hospitals off and on, and died at 49. Bertha Toftey, my mom's eldest sister, who lived to be almost 105 years old, wrote a booklet called *Groszvater Kretzschmar's Pult*. In it she describes a startling family episode:

> While [father] was trying to do some gardening on a hot summer day, an epileptic seizure frightened everyone. When he recovered, he became frantic and tried to crank the Ford. When it would not start, he tried to push the car from the small garage. Mother could not dissuade him just to leave the car alone and to go into the house and rest. One of the children ran over to the neighbor's home. They came, and it was decided that he needed to go to the hospital.

Who could have guessed that taking him to the hospital on that hot summer day would extend to a hospital stay of seven years?

Mom was the third of six children who were supported by their mother, Josephine, an absolutely amazing person. She worked at a hospital in Rochester; cleaned private homes on the weekend; and raised six educated, solid children, all of whom went on to lead productive lives with successful families. I remember my father discouraged my mom from having grandmother at our home. Unfortunately, my siblings and I did not grow to appreciate this marvelous woman enough—after all, she helped shape my mother into the strong, smart woman she became.

As a senior in high school, Mom was on a six-member

Rochester debate team. Debate must have been an important activity then because there were 140 debate teams in the state and the contests were regularly reported in local newspapers, like high school sports today. Rochester's team moved through the tournament process and qualified for state competition. At the state tournament level, each school could only field three debaters. Mom was chosen along with two guys. In the state championship, Rochester debated the Ortonville team of three boys. Rochester won. I have the newspaper clippings she saved to commemorate the win. Mom had a natural curiosity and desire to learn, which she never lost. Along with that, she was logical and rational. I imagine she was a tough debater in her low-key way.

My strong-minded, hard-working father was born on May 20, 1910, in New York City to Russian-born Jewish immigrants. His father, Elias, eventually settled in Duluth, Minnesota, where Dad, his brothers Harry and Jacob, and his sister, Rebecca, were raised. While little is known of Dad's mother, who died in child-birth, we know he had a stepmother named Ida, but little else about her or the details of his childhood.

My father's life was hard at an early age. He didn't talk about it much at all. As outgoing as he was, he rarely spoke about growing up. Most of that information I had to piece together from my mother, and my uncle Harry, my father's oldest brother. In fact, what I consider one of the most important historical points about the Schneiderman family, I didn't find out until after my father's death on April 16, 1988.

Unfortunately, Uncle Harry passed away on February 25, 2002. There is so much I wish I had asked him. We spent a lot of time together, but I didn't ask about our family's past—in part because I was trained to believe you couldn't trust anything Harry said. I took his word with a proverbial grain of salt. I'll never forget an Easter Sunday dinner my wife, Sheila, and

I shared in the mid-1990s with my brother Russell, his wife, Monica, Uncle Harry, and three other family members.

At one point, Harry said to Russ and me, ". . . you know your name isn't really Schneiderman, it's Mintczer."

"Oh, is that right, Harry?" I said laughingly, knowing Russ and I were about to get into one of his *stories*.

Harry continued, "Mintczer was my dad's name, and so your dad's name, too. Our dad came over from Germany in 1905 and couldn't speak English very well." I later learned he was actually from Russia, but came to America via Germany. "So when they asked him his name," Harry continued, "he said *Schneiderman* because he thought they asked, 'What did you do for a living?' *Schneiderman* means *tailor man*. So, he became Eli Schneiderman, but his real name was Elias Mintczer."

Russ joked, "Oh yeah! Then we need to change all the signs on our stores to Mintczer's."

Later, my mom confirmed the tale. "Yeah, yeah, that's true," she said matter-of-factly, as if we should all know.

"And you never thought it was important enough to mention to us?" I said. I was flabbergasted that she didn't share my view of the importance of the information. "Our name isn't really our name?"

"I guess not."

That's how, without much thought, Mintczer became Schneiderman. Just think, today people could be buying their furniture from Mintczer's and not Schneiderman's. Perhaps something as simple as an unchanged last name could have meant our stores would never have existed at all.

My dad did tell me his family had lived in Duluth while he was growing up, and that he only finished the eighth grade. I know that much. Unfortunately, there are more blanks than concrete information about my dad's early years. There was more he wanted to forget about those early days than he wanted to remember.

As the story goes, my paternal grandmother died during childbirth with my dad in May 1910. We don't know much about the next couple of years, except that my grandfather eventually remarried. Harry said his stepmom didn't like Harry, Jake, and my dad much. He said she was mean, possibly abusive. However, we have to remember this *was* Harry speaking. The boys were sent to live in an orphanage for a short period, though we don't know why. Harry said it was because their father couldn't handle the boys easily after his wife's death. A more likely scenario is that Eli couldn't find work in New York, and he headed west. He settled in Duluth, and he eventually sent for his sons. However it happened, they were a New York family in Duluth.

And that is where my parents met.

The beginning of my parents' relationship had a simple enough start—a blind date, according to my mother. My father joked that he didn't even want to go on it. "But, look where it got us," my mom would say.

Yes, look where it got them: six children and a small store started in the middle of nowhere that left behind a big legacy. During most of their life together, they did what they had to do. They were unconventional, with bouts of spontaneity, and whatever came along, they pushed through it.

This 1957 entry from my mother's journal offers her perspective on the early days of their marriage:

> *Before the store, I was going through nurse's training, and had two years of college in the Twin Cities, so of course I had no trouble getting in there at all.*
>
> *I was a nursing student in Saint Luke's Hospital and a friend of Max's invited him over to her house.*
>
> *I don't know how or why I started going with him. My friend was trying to set us up. He was interested after seeing me*

working in the nursing home, I guess.

You couldn't be married if you were in the nurse's training, nor could teachers at St. Luke's. It wasn't unusual there to have such stupid rules. You definitely couldn't be married; we knew this. We did get married, though.

Max went out in the summer time every three months for the Naval Reserve. He had training then.

When I first met him, I thought, "This isn't a good guy for you." I didn't fall for him at all at first. He was a New Yorker. I liked him, but my family didn't meet him until after we were married. Nobody was supposed to know we were together. They assured us it wouldn't be in the paper or anything like that because my friend knew the person in the paper and they said, "No, of course it won't be in the paper."

We were so innocent. Stupid.

I knew darn well Max wasn't a good guy for me, so I was probably in love with him right away.

I'm sure my parents didn't want me to marry Max. I don't know why. He wasn't Lutheran, but I don't think that was the reason, although it may have played into it.

Like I said, we got married and no one was supposed to know it. That was the problem.

It wasn't until we were married quite a while [that] St. Luke's found out. We thought we had gotten by okay. I'd been working quite a while, in spite of it. I didn't think anybody knew it. Oh, I was so stupid.

I was called in one day, and the head trainer said, "I hate to do this, but you cannot be in training when you are married." They were so strict. "I hate to do this, but it's impossible."

It was hard. I'd already had a couple years of college and, of course, I thought I'd gotten along just fine. It was easy for me at the school training.

We'd gotten married anyway, even though I wasn't allowed

to. I was married in a Lutheran church, in the parsonage. I [didn't] have anybody come to the wedding.

I wasn't really trained right growing up. My father was dead early at 48. I should have had more, I don't know . . . I kind of did what I wanted to.

Mom was only 17 years old when her father died, which was coincidentally the same age as my dad was when his father died. It was no wonder she felt as if she hadn't been well trained growing up. I can't imagine the person I would have become if I'd lost either of my parents at such an early age. At 17 I was only just coming into my own and discovering my love for the store. Mom had lost a parent.

Mom's journal is a simple coil-bound notebook that likely came from our own store in 1957, priced at 25 cents. Her first entry was recorded nine years after my parents opened the store. The next entry is dated September 29, 1981. She writes:

Here it is 24 years later. My good intentions of keeping a diary didn't work out. When I read my first attempt, it sounded pretty young and naive, but really, at almost 69 I don't feel any wiser. We just had our 46th wedding anniversary and we both feel we've been fortunate [to have] a lot more plusses than minuses. One thing, I wish we had been able to communicate better all these years. I envy people who can sit down and discuss things without any animosity. Are there really such people?

I flip through the notebook occasionally. The pages are yellowing, a small water or coffee stain leaves colored impressions on an inside corner, and I can't help but feel my family's history on these few pages. The journal's pages cover my parents' history in eight more entries, written over a span of 31 years. They reflect on some of the worst times my family has been through. From the death of my brother Russell's son Joey at age five of lymphoblastic leukemia, to the final entry on May 20, 1988, one month and four days after my father's death.

Our life before 1948, before storekeeping, seems really long ago. We enjoyed our life together in a different way. Our earliest married years were probably the most traumatic—the thrill of being in love, kind of a two-against-the-world feeling. Love conquers all soon collided with reality.

A paycheck on two days every other week was impossible for inexperienced me. And when I ran up a grocery bill of $50.00, it was a major disaster. Good thing Max didn't mind taking any kind of job, even carrying coal on his shoulders. We learned. We survived, and even enjoyed our life. Can you visualize Max pushing a baby buggy around Leif Erikson Park? He did—seems strange now that our pediatrician, Dr. Nutting, didn't ever tell us Dave, our firstborn, would probably be retarded.

When I look at his baby picture, wow, it seems pretty obvious.

So, we lived in a fool's paradise for a brief time. After Karen was born in 1938, we had two babies to care for, I didn't think I'd ever want another child. Thank heavens Karen was bright and beautiful and a good child—stubborn, but okay. How I ever had the nerve to board a train with a two-year-old, and a helpless four-year-old, and go to New York really astounds me now. That year in New York was really okay. Sure, I was lonesome when Max was at sea in the Navy, but the two children kept me busy and they really [needed] a lot of attention. I had a lovely neighbor in the upstairs apartment. She and I sat in front of the radio together when we heard about Pearl Harbor. When Max's ship came in, he got orders to go to Norfolk, Virginia, and that really upset me. I remember he mixed me a few stiff drinks, but I just cried harder. My cousins in Brooklyn helped tide me over [during] that lonesome time in New York. Then it was on to Norfolk with my two children.

We always had nice places to live, which many Navy wives didn't. Some had to live in one-room apartments for months. The years in Norfolk were quite interesting . . . that is after our furniture finally came in from New York. We were in a Navy project, so neighbors loaned us the bare essentials for those weeks. Service people certainly have a special camaraderie you don't experience elsewhere.

We babysat each other's children, had car pools to the commissary, coffee'd together, and comforted each other when our men had to leave. In spite of the war, those three and a half years weren't bad.

For one whole year, Max taught damage control at the base and was home every night. I would have liked that arrangement for the duration, but Max got "antsy" and off he went on a minesweeper. He was a Warrant Officer now and next to the captain in pay. Family time allowances were great. It was not like when he first left Duluth on the Paducah and I had to go to the Red Cross for some tiding over money. That was hard. As I recall, the Navy kept a whole month's pay for uniforms and we had no savings.

First, I went to the welfare office and I'm glad the man who interviewed me suggested I go to the Red Cross. If we had gotten aid from welfare, it would have been on record and we wouldn't have liked that—poor, but proud. How times have changed.

Norfolk especially goes down in history for two events— my bad bout of pneumonia and the birth of Phillip in 1944. I vividly remember the frustration of my illness. It was holiday time, and Max had trouble getting a doctor to come see me.

When he finally succeeded, I was in an ambulance and taken across the bay to the Navy hospital in a hurry. It took a long time before I felt 100% okay again.

The next trip to the hospital to have Phillip was much more pleasant. Phil wasn't exactly a beautiful baby at birth, but, in a few months, he was a doll, with his curly hair and crooked smile.

Karen started school in Norfolk. I'll never forget that day when she came home from school, because I had the door hooked and she couldn't get in pronto, she had an accident. She was furious with me, so embarrassed.

One Christmas in Norfolk was really memorable. All fall, every available evening after the children were in bed, Max worked on bunk beds and an armoire for Karen's dolls. He had found some beautiful wood at the base and worked hard to finish them by Christmas. I sewed clothes for her doll, even little boots, and a skating outfit—hard to believe!

One of Max's crew was a bar keeper in civilian life and he did the bar keeping while I fixed dinner for Max's whole crew one holiday. My older sister, Bertha, sent us a small evergreen from Grand Marais, MN, over Christmas and though it was pretty dry, it thrilled us.

Springtime in Norfolk was special. I loved those azaleas. Then Max got orders to go to the Pacific and he didn't tell me until the night before he was leaving. That was a "rainy" night, and some pretty lonely days.

The end of the war came while he was in the Pacific. When Max got back to Norfolk we called a friend in Morgan Park and asked him to buy us a house. We were lucky he could buy part of a triplex, or "sheep shed" as they were called; a house divided into three apartments.

Max said he wouldn't go back to the steel plant, but it was that or stay in the Navy. We were a little tired of Navy life, so back we went to Minnesota. We had another long wait for our furniture and I was pregnant again, this time with Claudia in November of 1945. Back to the steel plant for Max and just in time to walk a picket line, which he hated to do, since he hadn't even voted for the strike.

Though her journal doesn't make this point explicitly, my understanding is that the most significant reason for the return to Duluth was David, who they were told wouldn't live past his teenage years. Had David not been handicapped, there would be no Schneiderman's Furniture today, because Dad would have stayed in the Navy. Given David's challenges, though, he chose to leave the Navy and return to a civilian job at U.S. Steel.

After 21 years at the steel mill, where he worked in the nail mill, my father was tired of it. He didn't have any specific complaints. They liked living in Morgan Park, a planned community built in Duluth, Minnesota, in the early 1900s by U.S. Steel. At one time U.S. Steel had 5,000 employees in Duluth and the Morgan Park neighborhood was essentially the company town. Dad had worked long enough to collect his pension, and he no longer wanted to work for someone else. He wanted his own business. It didn't matter what that business was, he wanted to be the owner.

My father didn't talk much about his past. *The past was in the past*, he'd say—which was funny because if he had a grudge against someone, family, friend, or anyone else, he'd never forget it. He'd replay those stories over and over. One such grudge, and the only story I remember him telling about the mill, was about my brother David's cradle.

My dad was a pretty handy guy. During his spare time, he built a cradle for David and took a lot of pride in it. One day one of the supervisors noticed that Dad had built the cradle at work. The only thing was, Dad was a conscientious guy about work time and he'd made it during hours he was off the clock and using his own tools. The way Dad told the story, the supervisor said, "We don't do personal stuff while we're working." Impulsively, the man picked up the cradle, threw it to the ground, and smashed it into smithereens. My dad told me he cried when he saw it in pieces on the floor.

Actually, it was his supervisor's supervisor who destroyed the cradle. Dad's direct supervisor went off and talked to someone else about what had happened. When he came back, he told my dad he could rebuild the cradle on company time.

David was born in October 1936, so that cradle is now more than 70 years old. Incidentally, instead of having an arc on the bottom for rocking as it originally had, the cradle's bottom is cut off. I asked my mom about it. She laughed and said, "Oh, that!" Apparently mother's mother was staying with them for a while and my dad didn't like her staying with us. My grandmother was rocking David hour after hour upstairs. They could hear the creaking downstairs and it was driving my dad crazy. So, Dad took the cradle and cut the legs off so my grandmother couldn't rock him anymore.

I think the cradle incident and similar situations were symptoms of how the mill was run—and that led, or perhaps provoked, Dad to leave. He was a hard worker with a big mind and he needed to run things his way.

But he was ultimately compelled to quit when a sales representative position came up and he had applied for it. His supervisor told him, "Max, you do a great job in the nail mill, but you only have an eighth-grade education. You're never going to be a sales rep." After that, Dad was determined to quit. He started looking in the newspaper classifieds for opportunities.

My mom recalled, "When we looked in the newspaper and saw the advertisement, it was an old store they were advertising and somebody wanted a liquor license and couldn't have it or something. They had some kind of an incident there. The store owner shot a couple people. [Many of the people in Elmer] didn't want to come in the store for a long time."

I asked her why people wouldn't want to come in that store, and in her particular candid tone, she snapped back in defense of those people, "Would you like to go to a store where they shot someone?"

Dad hadn't thought about whether or not he wanted a store in downtown Duluth or out in the country—he just wanted a store of his own. One day he was waiting to go to work on the second shift when he saw an ad in the classifieds. He'd been scanning the classifieds since coming back from the Navy. He turned to my mom, "Let's go look at this place!"

"Not goin' to work?" Mom asked. It was unlike him because he was very conscientious. But that day he didn't go to the mill. They drove to Elmer and looked at the store, completely unaware at first that it had belonged to Joe Constanzi, the Elmer shooter.

"Why it appealed to us, I'll never know," said my mom decades later. "Except Max was so desperate to get out of that steel plant. He'd been gone five years with the Naval Reserve during the war and he always said, 'I'm not going back to that steel plant,' but we had four children and he needed a job, so where do you go? You go back. He was unhappy after he'd gotten back and after he'd been gone for so long. He wanted a store."

My understanding is that Dad wanted a business, not necessarily a store. He wanted anything where he could be his own boss and get out of the steel mill. The original store wasn't anything like it would be a decade later. When they first looked at the Constanzi store, it had less than $1,500 in inventory. There wasn't much hardware or many groceries. There wasn't much of anything! Later, Dad would say, "I must have been out of my mind to even consider the place."

It was the post office within the store that saved their lives the first few years because it was at least a little bit of steady income. Elmer is a rural township, not a town. Mom became Elmer's postmistress, which she operated until the U.S. Postal Service finally shut it down and she retired from her post on December 30, 1972. Once the Elmer post office was closed, our address changed to Meadowlands, which is a village about four miles away. Meadowlands was neither a cultural center nor a tourist town, but that's where we attended high school and where there were taverns, a gas station, churches, and a couple of grocery stores. When I was a kid, Meadowlands even boasted a movie theater and pool hall. Growing up in Elmer essentially meant growing up in Meadowlands. I think and speak of them almost interchangeably.

"My relatives thought buying the store was a good idea," Mom wrote in her journal. "That surprised me. And, it surprised me that Max listened to them. My mother and Max weren't real close, but she loaned us $5,000 for the down payment. That was a lot of money at the time." Until I began reading through Mom's letters, I had no idea my grandmother, Josephine Kretzschmar, loaned my parents the down payment money. I asked Mom how she had that much money to loan to Dad. She responded, "Darned if I know."

Apparently my grandmother's small nest egg had traveled to most of her children at one time or another and had always been paid back. Soon after lending the money to my parents, she decided she wanted to buy her first house and asked my parents for the money back. Dad went to the bank in Duluth and tried to borrow the money, and of course, they weren't going to lend him the money straight out. They sent him to the mortgage department, where he told the banker he had to borrow $1,500. When asked what the money was for, Dad told him, "To pay off my mother-in-law so she can buy a house."

The banker laughed. "Well, the bank can't give you the credit, but I'll give you a personal check for it." So he wrote out a check for $1,500, saying, "Any man *that* concerned about paying his mother-in-law back won't have a problem paying a bank back." My parents and their new enterprise got some nice breaks along the way. It didn't take my parents too long to prove their worth when it came to credit, and they borrowed money a lot.

They had purchased the small grocery on a whim, with my grandmother's help and money borrowed from friends. What hurt them most initially was that it wasn't until after they bought the place that they found out the previous owner had murdered all those people.

In one of her journal entries, Mom reflects on their choice:

It is strange how we are guided on such unexpected roads in life. If we had stopped and pondered the situation, we would never have bought the dilapidated, poorly stocked country store. We had half a dozen strikes against us before we even moved in. The prejudice against the place was widespread since the former owner shot three men in cold blood and wounded two more in frustrated anger against being denied an off-sale liquor license. Since the people in the area are closely interrelated, that was a dark cloud to dispel.

I remember how Max heaved a sigh of relief when he was finally able to dispose of the truck that belonged to the poor, demented soul. Then too, rural people are a little more unreasonable in some of their prejudices and we winced every time someone made an anti-Jewish remark. It was some time before we felt like discussing Max's racial heritage, but I think we worried needlessly on that account. Knowing Max, I should have known better. I've never seen a person who could sell himself as easily as Max, and that's been the biggest factor in our success. He is an exceptionally able salesperson and it never fails to interest me when I hear him launch into a sales talk.

I think after ten years all our friends and customers think of Max as "Max" their friend with no racial prejudice. How he ever succumbed to buying a rural store, I'll never know. Definitely, there's divine guidance in some of our decisions. I had lived in a rural community as a child in my father's parish, but, city boy Max had never been without the convenience of city life. But Max seemed unfazed, even when we were pumping water and carrying it up to our living quarters, and then carrying the slop water out again. Or, when we had to battle a storm to go out to that little leaky house in the rear, we enjoyed our life because it was our own—or would be after we repaid Mother and other friends.

I'm sure we never would have gotten such a tremendous kick out of a tidy little store in town. In our first five years, we worked seven days a week from 8:00 a.m. until 10:00 p.m., or later. We modernized our living quarters and made them comfortable, put a new front on the store, and built up our stock from $1,500 to about $10,000. I'm sure we would never have been able to make such progress in a city.

Max was willing to sell anything anyone ordered. If we didn't stock it, he'd shop for it. His list was quite a story in itself on some of his excursions. He'd shop everything from feed to clothing to meats to all the other items a general store wanted to have, to special requests for outlandish items like pine tar, goldfish, or memorial wreaths. Not only did he have to establish himself with his customers, but he had to gain entrance to dozens of sources of supply—right after World War II, some of the wholesalers weren't too anxious to take on an unknown rural shopkeeper with big ideas, but no cash.

After selling the store, Signe Constanzi moved into a tiny home next to the store, while my parents moved into the living quarters above the store with David, Karen, Phillip, and Claudia. To give you an idea of how deep into the boondocks they were, my parents were told to move into the store before April. If they waited until the snow melted, the roads would be too difficult to drive on because the ice would melt and turn the roads into mud. That was one of the first signs of the difficult times to follow.

Reflecting back on my parents' early years in Elmer, our family friend Frank Sramek told me that "Max was something different for the community. Naturally people would comment, wondering if he would be successful in operating a country store with no experience in this type of venture."

Where Joe Constanzi had been a typical Iron Ranger, strong and hardworking, he also had a chip on his shoulder and came across with attitude. Frank remembers that Joe seemed to just expect loyalty from the potential and regular customers in the surrounding area. He didn't take on extra measures to promote the store. My dad had a different way of doing business. He immediately established a new system at the store—if we don't have it in stock, I'll get it for you. My parents kept a range of brochures and catalogs available in the store for exactly this purpose. This policy expanded well beyond groceries as he built the store into hardware and eventually furniture. He was also ready to help with additional "favors," such as hauling items for people instead of driving with an empty truck. Along with my dad's new approach and my mother's talent for customer service, the new policy changed the way neighbors looked at the store.

Stigma and prejudice weren't the first problems my parents faced. The store was in shambles and falling apart even before they'd moved in. On top of that, many of the basic luxuries they thought they'd have were absent. They had to sell a car and make do with only a truck. When they moved in, the building lacked running water. When they initially looked at the place they saw a sink in the kitchen and assumed there was running water.

They had to go to neighbors' homes to get water to drink and use for washing and cooking. When they poured wastewater down the drain in the kitchen, it would come out near the shed. According to my mother, two elm trees were killed that way.

Their biggest disappointment was the toilet. The real estate guy told my parents they had a chemical toilet in the basement. So, Dad went down there to look at it, down these rickety stairs. He saw the toilet and didn't investigate further. It turned out it was only a toilet seat over a five-gallon can. My mom would repeat over and over through the years, "We were so dumb."

They had almost nothing when they started the store. According to my mom, I was "the egg baby." She explained that "the local farmers brought their eggs to the store for us to buy and resell. We had to check each egg to make sure it was okay to sell. You have to put the eggs in front of the candle to check them. When Larry was born, we paid St. Luke's [Hospital] with eggs. So, he was called the egg baby. It took a while to pay them off."

But when Mom came home from the hospital after my birth, Dad had something for her that made it all worth it. He'd put in running water. It was the perfect homecoming present.

3

Work, Faith, and David

In 1988, when I was 39 years old, my dad was seriously ill with diabetes and his medication had ravaged his body. It was a struggle for him to even talk. Word had gotten around in the community that Max Schneiderman was dying. I was at work one day when I got a call from the pastor at the local Assembly of God church. We had known each other for years, as members of the two local Lutheran churches. I respected him, but harbored some mixed feelings after he left our church during the Charismatic Movement, taking others with him. Several years had passed since then, though. As I listened to him on the phone, I could tell he was a little nervous. He asked me if Pastor Julie, the minister of the church I attended, had been out to see my father. Well, no, she hadn't, but it wasn't her fault. My dad made it very plain he was not interested in having any minister come out to preach to him. In fact, as far as we knew, Dad was agnostic and quite negative in his view of religion and churches.

The pastor told me, "God has laid on me His will that I go

and talk to your dad." Well, in fact, I do believe God does this at times, so I said, "Let me go talk to him and I'll call you back."

At the time, my parents were living in a brick home they'd built in 1967, which was just around the corner from the store. So I went over to see him, and said, "A friend of mine wants to pray with us. What do you think? Would you be okay with that?"

He turned his head toward me slowly, stared at me for a moment, and said, "Are you nuts?" Those were the last words Dad said to me before he died.

Deep in my heart, because of my own faith, I hope my father wasn't agnostic. All the evidence suggests he was, though. What little I know of his early years leads me to believe he had his reasons.

My father and both of his parents, from the standpoint of faith, and by background, would have been Jewish. But Dad wasn't raised Jewish and he didn't know anything about being a Jew. He said he didn't believe in God. It further complicated matters that my mom was the daughter of a Missouri Synod Lutheran minister. My mother, even from a young age, was more open-minded than either of her parents. Yet, she remained devoted to her faith. Mom's family, in Dad's mind, had "religiosity" that was off the charts and they seemed opposed to him. They made it clear that they didn't want my mother to go with him, because according to them, he'd never amount to anything. It didn't help that they knew he wasn't a Christian. I think their attitudes further divided my father from wanting any relationship with religion.

The agreement my mother and father made was that my father would never go to church, but he would support raising me and my siblings in the Lutheran church. Both of my parents stuck to the deal. Later in life, though, my mother told me she wished she hadn't made that covenant with my dad—she wished she could have influenced him, or tried to influence him.

In fact, when I was younger and I had somehow gotten the

idea from church, I challenged him about his beliefs. The Bible says you are supposed to go and "make disciples," and people at our church were not particularly strong in that direction, *for which many were thankful.* It bothered me that Dad didn't believe as Mom and I did, so I raised the topic one day when he and I were out driving down some long road on our way to measure carpeting for a customer. I remember this so vividly. We were driving between the towns of Virginia and Hibbing, when I ventured to start talking to him about God. He pulled the car over to the side of the road, eased off the shoulder, shut the motor off, put his index finger in my face, and said, "Do not talk to me about a God! If there was a God there wouldn't be people like your brother David!" The anger in my dad's face that day was incredible. I never tried to convince my dad about faith again.

David was born mentally handicapped, and in those days, people like him were put in homes. But my mom and dad were tremendous with David. They were caring, protective, and patient. Dad always preferred to keep David close. There was a time earlier in David's life when Mom wanted to try out an institutional setting for him. Though David enjoyed it, my parents had a hard time with him being away. Not letting David live with other handicapped kids is something Mom regrets, but I don't think my dad ever did. They were told he wouldn't live beyond his teen years, but as I write this in 2013, David is 77 years old. As I teased my mother, you know you're old when you have a 77-year-old kid.

While I was growing up, I didn't realize what a gift David was. All my brothers and sisters are comfortable around people with disabilities. If you haven't spent a lot of time around handicapped people, it's normal and natural to feel uncomfortable, because it can make you uneasy. David says and does some weird and unpredictable things. One thing he does all the time is repeat what he's saying. He'll repeat it over, and over, and over until you answer him. If he doesn't receive an answer he can accept, he'll continue to repeat himself. Sometimes it drives the people at the nursing home where he lives now to distraction. I know it does, but my mother doesn't understand that.

One day my wife and I were visiting with David at the nursing home and a visitor came in who caught his attention. She was dressed in all white. He said, "Hello, nurse. Hello, nurse." The woman in white had no idea he was addressing her because she wasn't a nurse. I was trying to distract him, but I wasn't succeeding, which wasn't unusual. Then one of the attendants at the nursing home came by and asked if I was going to bring David to bingo. He loves bingo!

"Sure, where is it?" I asked.

As I was wheeling him through the hall, he was still doing this "Hello, nurse. Hello, nurse" thing. Finally, the woman realized when we were passing by her that he was addressing her. She said, "I'm sorry. I'm not a nurse, I'm a visitor."

So then he started, "Hello, visitor. Hello, visitor." Those kinds of things are fun for a short time, but they can be exhausting!

His routines are unbelievable. If my mom got him used to taking a vitamin in the morning, he would say, "Vitamin, vitamin, vitamin." He'd do that all day long until you gave it to him. He's a huge routine guy. He has to do the same things, the same way, every time.

David probably has the intellect of a three-year-old in most ways. His brain was damaged in childbirth. He's not capable of a normal conversation, but he has certain routine questions. When he sees me, he'll get a big, loving smile on his face and say, "Larry Alan."

He'll continue to say my name like that until I say, "David Max."

Then he'll say, "What kind of car do you drive?"

I taught him to say, "Lexus. Damn imports." (Even though

my mom always shook her head when she heard him say "damn.") And he laughs because he's used to people laughing at his one-liner.

It's incredible how much music he knows. I can play a few bars of a song and he'll know what it is. It is one of his favorite games, which was a great discovery for me, and makes visiting him a lot more enjoyable. He loves the older music—like Al Jolson, Ella Fitzgerald, Frank Sinatra, and Dean Martin. I'll ask him what he wants to listen to, and then I'll put it on the iPhone or iPad. It is a marvel for him. Sometimes I'll find songs on YouTube that include the lyrics in subtitles. He can read along, and he loves that. We don't know how much he retains, but Mom taught him to read and he loves reading children's books. True to his need for routine, when David comes to a word he doesn't know, he'll ask, "What is this? What is this?" He'll say it over and over until someone tells him the word.

When he sees me these days, after we do the "Larry Alan" and the "damned Lexus," he'll say, "Where's your iPhone? Where's your iron pad?" (That's what he calls my iPad.) It's a riot watching him use the "iron pad" because it almost looks as if he's using the thing to check his email. The nursing home staff—most know him well—give David a second look when they see him, because it's a little out of context to see him using this iPhone or iPad, playing with it.

Mom and David lived in the same nursing home in Duluth. Few things made my mom angry, and she didn't cry often. But, one incident made her so angry she was in tears while sharing the story with me. The nursing home has Catholic roots, and some of the staff are nuns. David loves going to mass and my mom would go with him. He loves to receive communion, which he calls the "bread of life" because my mother would call it that. One day they got a new priest.

The practice of the Catholic church is that you cannot take

communion unless you are Catholic and have confessed your sins. So, the priest refused to give David communion. David was crying, "I want the bread of life. I want the bread of life." The guy absolutely refused to do it. My mother was incredibly angry with him. Now the nursing home has Protestant services, and David can again experience the "bread of life" again.

While David can be exasperating, he has a degree of love you don't find in others. When I say goodbye to David (he's in a wheelchair), he always puts his arm around me or I'll put my head down against his. He's a warm, loving person. David is a blessing for the whole family. As Mom noted her spiral notebook shortly after my dad's passing, "Max has been gone from our circle for a month and four days and that empty feeling will persist for some time, I'm sure. Thank God for Dave. He keeps full the void so very much."

Growing up in Duluth, before the family's move to Elmer township, Dave attended elementary school for a brief time. A bus would pick him up and take him to Jefferson School near St. Luke's Hospital, and then my parents had to fetch him at noon. Since he wasn't able to go to the bathroom by himself, the school staff felt they were making quite a concession in taking him *that* long. Handicapped care has come a long way. I can't say his short exposure to formal education did him much good, but my parents tried.

My brother Russell and I alternated weeks taking care of David. One of us had to get David ready in the morning, which meant dressing him, shaving him, and giving him breakfast. The other had duties in the grocery store—taking all the rubbish out, changing all the calendars, sweeping, and putting up the flag. Phil did the heavy-lifting chores—organizing materials in the storage area: roofing, corrugated tin, iron pipe, hundred-pound sacks of animal feed, salt blocks, and bags of cement mix. So, he spent time in the storage area putting things away and organizing. My sisters Karen and Claudia did everything we did with David, and probably more.

At one time, Russ, David, and I all shared a bedroom. It was difficult sleeping in there with David because of his repetition habit. He would pick some word and repeat it over, and over, and over again. It seemed as if he never slept. Russ and I would talk about that all the time. No matter what time David went to bed it seemed like he was always sitting up. During the day, he would sit at the front window and watch customers come into the store. We had gas pumps out there. He'd watch customers fill up with gas.

My mom has said she feels guilty about David and the life she was able to give him. I don't think she should have carried that guilt. She wondered whether they could have found someplace that would have been more stimulating for him. She thought of him as this poor kid sitting up there all day watching the front of the store. I don't see it that way at all.

Due to our age differences, my siblings and I were more like three families than one. David and Karen were the oldest, and then you had a number of years until Phil and Claudia, and then the two youngest, Russ and me. I think my mom and dad were different parents to each pair. They were probably better parents for Russ and me than for the others. Perhaps they learned some things raising my four older siblings, or maybe it was a little easier because they were no longer struggling financially, or both. Despite the differences in how we were raised, the five youngest of us had three constants that always remained important: work, faith, and David.

As hectic as our household was in the morning, with all of the kids trying to get ready for the school bus, we would still say a psalm and a prayer together each morning. As a dad myself, I am amazed when I think back on how my mother managed to carve out that special time for prayer each morning—both because of the number of kids she was managing, and everything else we had going on. Sometimes the bus had to wait for us, but she always made time for the prayers.

At the visitation before my father's funeral, a man who wasn't very close to our family approached me and commented, "I will always think there is a place in Heaven for your mother and father for what they did with David." It was nice he noticed enough to say something. Not only did my parents not institutionalize David at a time when that was the common choice for handicapped children, but they also included him as an important part of our family. It was an exceptional accomplishment and I respect them for their care of David. I think he has lived a pretty good life.

My brother Russ once told me, "David's come a long way. When we were growing up he was retarded; then he became handicapped; now he's special." I'll always remember that.

Perhaps partly as a result of her experiences with my brother David, Mom was extremely open-minded and never judgmental. I always admired that about her. I think she always had a liberal feminist streak in her and to the very end had some negative feelings toward the Missouri Synod Lutheran Church, which remains extremely conservative. Long before homosexuality was understood and accepted as more mainstream, she was open toward gay people. Before my brother Phil's son Greg became ill and died of AIDS, she flew out to California to meet Greg's partner. Like me, Mom had a hard time with the conservative church that wanted to isolate and segregate people who are different. The way my mother looked at it is when His followers asked Jesus what the greatest commandment was, He answered, "Love God with your whole heart, soul, and mind." When they asked Him what the second greatest commandment was, He answered, "Love your neighbors as you would yourself." How can you justify being unwelcoming to any group when Jesus said that? That's the way my mother felt, and so do I.

4

First Lessons from My Dad

Perhaps fittingly, the family couch led to the beginning of Schneiderman's Furniture.

Well, let me step back a little. At first in their new store, my parents were primarily in the grocery and hardware business—and to be honest, they weren't really making a go of it. They needed a couch for the family, but didn't have the money to pay for it. So, Dad got a job part-time at Marshall-Wells, a wholesale furniture business in Duluth where he bought the couch. At one time Marshall-Wells was the largest wholesale business in the world and that was Dad's first exposure to the furniture business. More importantly, that's where he got the idea to put a few pieces of furniture in the store and have people order from a catalog, saving them quite a bit of money without the high overhead. It's like the way people use the Internet today, or think they do.

My dad had a compelling personality. Everyone he met fell into one of two categories: those who liked him, and those who didn't relate to him. But there were always *more* people who liked him. He had a lot of personality. He was funny and it was fun to conduct business with him. He quoted a low price right from the start, leaving people no room to bargain lower for a better deal. But he was extremely rigid. There was no negotiation. I mean zero. It wouldn't be unusual for someone to see a $1,000 sofa on sale for $800 in Duluth. Then they'd come to my dad's store and his price was $650. That was that, period. No matter how much a person bought, or how long they were a customer, there was no negotiation with him. Still today, but especially then, people would often try to get additional discounts. One guy said to my dad, "If I buy this and this, would you throw in that?" Dad replied, "I won't throw anything in, but I'll throw up if you want me to." That was the way he would do things, with a joke. Either people would laugh and be won over, or they just didn't get it. This particular guy laughed and that was the end of it. Humor aside, it's almost always wise to figure out a way not to say "no" to a customer. Dad's way was unique to him.

Dad also had his own sense of right and wrong, his own moral code. I suppose we all do. He knew what was in his code and what was not. One of Dad's core beliefs is that everybody should pay the same price. It was more than a business philosophy—it was his moral statement.

Only once, and I think he regretted it until he died, did Dad give in. He was working with a particularly difficult customer. During the buying process, the guy told Dad, "If I buy from you today, you're going to throw in that lamp." The customer mentioned the lamp a couple more times while he was shopping. He had a big order so when he presented the final bill, Dad figured out a way to keep true to his code that everyone pays the same price. He was ready when the guy demanded again that the lamp be thrown in for free. Dad "threw in" the lamp, but added the price of the lamp onto another item, rationalizing that he was still cheaper on the item than other stores. Dad remembered an uncomfortable feeling of being true to his moral code, but less than honest about the price of the lamp, and he brought up the incident many times over the years. He regretted agreeing to throw in the lamp, because he thought that kind of sales tactic leads to dishonesty.

Pricing was a big thing for Dad—both good and bad. The good thing is he would provide a low price. The bad part was his insistence on no negotiations, well before nonnegotiable pricing became familiar. It has become more common for businesses, most recently the car industry, to offer no-hassle, nonnegotiable prices. That's what Dad offered 60-plus years ago. His stand on the issue is the starting point for a number of family stories. One that sticks with me involves Bill Krueger, a well-known radio and television personality in the Duluth area, and his wife. They were nice people. They were interested in a Henredon sofa, which is a high-end brand that's still around. (The furniture business gains and loses manufacturers all the time.) The Kruegers really liked the sofa, but they didn't like that it wasn't available in a certain fabric they'd seen in our store. We didn't sell the Henredon brand, but we were doing some business with a small Minneapolis manufacturer with incredibly high standards called Livon Manufacturing. My dad was friends with the owner, Marshall Livon, who later became a friend of mine as well. Dad showed Marshall a picture of this Henredon sofa and asked him if he could make it. It had a decorative scalloped-type skirt and was very distinctive. Marshall said he could and commented on how he could go even further with the detailing. But Dad said he wanted the sofa to look exactly like the Henredon style. In our business, today more than then, it isn't uncommon to see similar styles from one manufacturer to another. Marshall said he would make the sofa with a better construction than the Henredon, which might or might not have been true. The

Kruegers had been quoted about $2,000 for the Henredon sofa, and that was a long time ago.

"With our usual margin we could sell the Livon sofa for $880," Dad told me. "What price do you think I tell the Kruegers?"

"How do you know they're going to buy it?" I asked. "Maybe they're going to want one with the Henredon name on it."

"No, no," he assured me. "I think they'll want to buy it from us."

"Well, you're going through a lot of extra trouble. The thing is highly customized. If they change their mind, what are you going to do with it? I think you're justified to sell it at a higher price."

Without another word to me about it, Dad picked up the phone, called Mrs. Krueger, and said, "It will be $880." He wanted to make a point to me.

The Kruegers were thrilled; they bought the sofa and became great customers of ours. They knew many people in Duluth and sent them right over to us. I can imagine Bill Krueger talking about seeing the Henredon at our competitor, Enger and Olsen, which is no longer in business, then bragging, ". . . and I got it at Schneiderman's for $880."

When I was around 15 years old, Dad expected me to sell furniture in the store every weekend. I was a good sales consultant and knew a lot about furniture. I mean I really loved furniture. I read everything I could find on the subject. I guess I was a "furniture geek." When the new catalogs came in, I was all over them.

One evening, my dad was trying to help a couple with specific tastes as they were describing a chair and ottoman they liked. They told my dad it was called a Charles Eames. Now, that type of contemporary, mid-century chair is more popular today than it was back then. A contemporary store, like Room

& Board, would have a version of the Eames chair on display, even today. But my dad had never heard the name and thought it was a name brand and told him, "Well, I've never heard of the brand."

The guy said, "Well, it's not a brand, it's a classic contemporary design."

Dad was doing the best he could. He went through the catalogs with chairs and couldn't find it. Finally, he saw me and asked, "Larry, have you ever heard of a Charles Eames chair?"

I said, "Yeah, I have."

"Have you ever seen it in any of our catalogs?"

"Yeah, Heywood-Wakefield makes one." They're another American furniture company no longer in existence.

So we got the catalog, and there it was. My dad looked at me, and I still remember his expression of pride and wonderment.

My brother Russell is a year and a half younger than I am. Because we were so close in age, it was common for us to receive duplicate or combined gifts. One Christmas we both got football helmets and shoulder pads. Another year Dad surprised us by having our brother Phil put up a rim and backboard to go with a new basketball. Russ and I did everything together in the summers. As in any small town, there wasn't much for kids to do in nearby Meadowlands, except hang out, or play sports. Luckily Russ and I both loved sports. In summer, we organized pick-up games with our friends. We both played basketball on the high-school team.

By then, our grocery and hardware business had grown and Dad had expanded the furniture store. Twice a week, Dad would hire someone to go with him to deliver furniture. Then once the truck was empty, he would stock up on groceries and hardware and bring them back to the store. Every night, Russ and I had our duties in the grocery store, but twice a week we also loaded the truck with my dad. On those two nights, Russ and I would come home from basketball practice, gulp down something for dinner, stock the grocery shelves, load the truck with furniture, and then do our homework. It might be 11:00 p.m. or midnight before we were finished.

Dad didn't have any full-time employees at this point. One day I caught wind that my dad was thinking about hiring some help. I was hoping he would. So I finally worked up the courage to talk to him about these two nights a week of loading. My dad was intimidating, but I can only remember him physically spanking me twice. The threat was always imminent, though. When he would get upset, he'd grab his belt and hitch it up. That was enough to scare us.

"You know, Dad," I began, "Russ and I come home from basketball practice. We grab something to eat, and we stock the shelves. Then we help you load the truck. It gets late and then we do our homework. Our grades are suffering."

I was pleasantly surprised that there was no pants-hitching. He said, "Alright, let me think about it."

I was feeling pretty smart. The next day I went to school. As I was walking in, the coach came up to me and asked, "What's going on? Your dad called and said you're no longer on the team. He said you're supposed to go right home after school and not to stay for practice."

"What?" I gasped. I waited until I could call my dad and talk to him in private. I had to call from the school office phone. I asked him what was going on.

He said he didn't want to talk about it then, that we'd talk about it when I got home. He ended the call with "I'm busy. Goodbye."

When I got home, I asked again, "What's going on?"

"Well, Larry, you told me your grades are suffering."

"It's not because of basketball practice, it's because of loading the truck."

He shot me a sarcastic look and said, "Play is optional. Work is something we have to do. Your grades are way more important than basketball."

So I spent the next ten minutes trying to convince him I could handle everything. He said, "So, you can play basketball—and you can do your other work, load the truck, and still do your homework and your grades are going to be okay?"

"Yeah! Yeah!"

"And I'm never going to hear about this again am I?" His eyes were twinkling.

"No!"

"Okay, you're back on the team."

My parents had five children working in and out of the store over the years. All of us are different. We must have driven Mom nuts all the time. But in her journal she reflects happily, "Larry and Russell would play basketball over the drapes. They would make a big ball of tinfoil and play basketball." We used the valance of the kitchen drapes as our basket. Our enthusiastic jump shots would make so much noise you could hear us in the store below. One night Russ and I had a friend stay overnight and the game got a little rough and I put my hand through the window and had to be rushed to the hospital for stitches.

Freelance writer Jane Brissette interviewed my parents for a story that appeared in the *Duluth News Tribune* in the 1980s. In the audio-taped interview, Mom and Dad offer a candid, and humorous, perspective:

EDNA. We had those two, Larry and Russell, after the other four. I didn't know what was wrong with our birth control.

MAX. There just wasn't anything to do up there.

EDNA. There were a lot of people in that place upstairs. At the time, it didn't seem like it. You do what you gotta do. I would sit outside and all I would think was "this is ours right now." And I was happy.

Until Karen left home, there were eight of us living in the small apartment above the store. We had one bathroom, which also doubled as the laundry room. Mom was in charge of the grocery and hardware sections of the store, in addition to her postmistress duties. She also took care of six kids, one of whom was severely handicapped. With all of her daily responsibilities, Mom didn't have any spare time. My brother Russ had difficulty reading and somebody at the school told my mom if Russ didn't improve, perhaps he should be held back a grade. So Mom committed herself to listening to him read aloud to her for an hour every day. I can still remember her ironing clothes in the store while Russ sat there reading to her. Later in life, Russ felt he had some degree of dyslexia, but at the time I'm not sure people understood the challenges it created for him.

Russ and I were inseparable growing up, but being older, I was out of the house first. That didn't stop us from hanging out, though. I remember I was in my first year of college up in the small town of Virginia, about an hour north of home, when Russ and a friend of his came to visit. Some bars in northern Minnesota were notorious for serving minors. Drinking was acceptable up there and we were in a bar called the Pickwick. I had a couple of my friends along and Russ had his friend with him. The high school principal from Toivola-Meadowlands High School, Val Melgeorge, and his wife came into the bar with another couple. Russ had always liked the guy, so Russ, who was only 18 at the time, ordered a round of drinks for them. Before I knew what was happening, Russ brought the drinks over to his principal's table.

The following Monday came around and Principal Melgeorge called Russ into the office. "I go into the Pickwick. I see you there. I try to ignore you, but you buy me drinks. You're ineligible for baseball. You can't drink and you can't be in a bar whether you're drinking or not. I tried to ignore you, but you wouldn't let me."

I think the incident taught Russ a pretty good lesson. And my dad wasn't too happy with me for bringing Russ into a bar and letting him drink. I'm sure he would have hitched his pants as he reprimanded me if I'd been home.

In our late teens, I was maturing too quickly and Russ was maturing in a more normal way. On weekends, we had responsibilities. Russ and I would work in the warehouse Saturday morning and I would sell in the store in the afternoon. Russ had no interest in working with customers and likely wondered why I wanted to.

Growing up, Russ and I were responsible for stacking and organizing the furniture and other stock in the warehouse. We always had more goods than we had space. Dad bought huge lots of things like sewing machines, building supplies, carpet, and the like. Russ and I were responsible for going out there and restocking inventory. I don't know if it was on a set schedule, but about once a month, we would clean up the warehouse and haul stuff to the dump. One day when I was still in high school, we had the truck nearly loaded with garbage. My dad was upstairs in bed with pneumonia and I went to ask him about an old green vinyl recliner with springs coming through the seat.

"What do you want us to do with it?" I yelled up the stairs.

"Throw it away! Throw it away!" he yelled back.

So we threw the recliner away with everything else. The next week I got a call at school over the intercom system. "Larry Schneiderman, please come to the office. Larry Schneiderman, please come to the office."

I went to the office, where I was told, "You're supposed to call your dad."

So, I called. "Dad, this is Larry. What would you like?"

"I'm looking for a green recliner and I remember you asking

me about it. Do you know where it is?"

I'm sure I was nervous when I replied, "Dad, you told us to throw it in the dump."

"That's what I was afraid of. Bye." It turns out Dad had picked up the green recliner to repair for somebody.

Now that he knew what we'd done with it, he headed to the dump to retrieve it. I didn't know it at the time, but in those days when the Schneiderman's truck made a delivery to the dump, sometimes there was a caravan of cars following it—the original Goodwill Store, if you will.

Well, someone had taken the green vinyl recliner. Dad had to contact its owners and tell them it wasn't repairable. "How about you buy any recliner I have, and I'll give you half off on it?"

The woman said, "That's a generous offer but I can't afford to buy anything so just bring it back to me."

"I was afraid you were going to say that," he said before confessing what had happened. He gave them a new recliner.

Years later, I was out with a friend of mine, a basketball teammate. I'd never been in his house before. We stopped at his place and when I walked in, I couldn't believe it. There was that green vinyl recliner with a cloth over the seat where the springs were poking through—sitting right in my buddy's living room! Talk about recycling. I could hardly wait to tell my dad.

Max Schneiderman had a one-of-a-kind personality and ribald sense of humor. One story that illustrates those attributes happened when my sister Karen was at that awkward age when anything our parents did embarrassed her.

At that point, the store carried a little of almost everything, including women's lingerie. A local customer who routinely bought groceries from us told Dad she wanted to buy a bra. Dad asked, "What size?"

She told him she didn't know.

So Dad said, "Well, let me get the measuring device." He walked over to the hardware department and brought back three different sizes of funnels and set them on the counter.

Karen ran upstairs yelling to Mom, "You won't believe what he is doing now!"

I'm guessing it wasn't easy being a teenage daughter of Max Schneiderman.

I don't remember much about Karen from my childhood years. She left home to attend nursing training when I was seven or eight. I do recall a period of time when she must have been responsible for looking after us. In fact, more than once I've heard Karen describe how she had to change my diapers—basically mother me. She also tells about how she found out Mom was going to have another baby brother. She was at church when an older lady asked, "So, your mother is pregnant again?"

Apparently she didn't take the news well because when she got home from church, she stormed upstairs, "Mom, how could you?"

I remember getting into some trouble once while Karen was watching us in church. During one of Pastor Thelander's lengthy sermons, Russ and I and two buddies from Sunday school broke out a deck of cards and started playing a card game called War. The elderly pastor noticed and stopped his sermon to admonish Karen for our behavior.

By the time she finished high school, Karen must have been more than ready to move on with her life. After completing her training, she became a registered nurse at the hospital in Virginia, Minnesota. While living there, she met and married Bob Braun. Russ and I were around twelve and ten at that time. We loved Bob. He played touch football with us and cracked us up with his humor and playfulness. Bob has a deep and pleasing tone of voice even today. He decided to become a radio announcer and worked in the industry for some years while Karen continued her nursing career in Illinois and Iowa. It must have been about 1968 or 1969 when Bob and Karen decided to move back to Meadowlands and work at Schneiderman's.

While Bob was employed at the store full time, Karen sold furniture part time. She had strong decorating skills and went on to get her ASID (American Society of Interior Designers) certification and eventually started her own business, Karen Interiors.

When Karen stopped working a schedule at the store, it left us short-handed, especially on Saturdays and Sundays. When Sheila offered to give sales a try, it surprised me a little. I knew she had what it takes, but she's on the quiet side and hadn't shown an interest in selling up to that point. In short order, she proved herself more than competent—she excelled. She started with flooring and once she became comfortable there, she expanded to the furniture side. Ultimately, she even learned the in-home design format and did very well. She particularly enjoyed working with the other salespeople. Eventually, the symptoms of rheumatoid arthritis made it too difficult for her to continue on the store's sales floor, but her experiences there helped her understand the business challenges we deal with.

Karen's husband, Bob, worked at Schneiderman's for 42 years, and he had many customers who enjoyed working with him. Both of Karen and Bob's sons, Jeff and Chris, worked in the Meadowlands warehouse during the summers. Both ultimately earned their college degrees, did well in the business world, and had strong families. Tragically, Jeff died at the age of 42 in a snow mobile accident. He was Mom's first grandchild.

After Karen left home, my sister Claudia, who would have been about 11 then, became responsible for making most of the meals. My family depended a lot on Claudia. Although I may not have noticed at the time, I know my parents both appreciated her for it. She was amazing. I asked my mom once when she had the time to teach Claudia to cook. Mom laughed and said she never did. Like everything else in our family in those days, if something had to get done, you just did it. Mom would supervise her, of course, saying things like, "You don't need to use that many dishes. You can cook this and that in the same pot, one after the other."

Early in her cooking days, Claudia announced, "If you want me to cook, then you need to let me do it my way!" So Mom kept her comments to occasional suggestions. They reached an agreement, and they stuck to it. Many summers we had construction workers around the building because we were adding on to the store. Claudia was responsible for meals for those guys too. I'm sure she was doing the housecleaning and helping with David, on top of her cooking. Like me, she was also active in the grocery store. Since she was older, she was depended upon more than I was for ringing up orders and packing groceries.

Claudia cooked and Russ and I had to do the dishes. Decades later, during my brother Russell's illness, I asked Claudia if she still uses every friggin' pot in the kitchen. It was one of our gripes growing up—why did she have to use every pot in the kitchen? She laughed, and said she still does. "Isn't it amazing that I still love to cook!" she added.

Wanting to continue reminiscing, I asked, "What's the first memory that comes to mind?"

Claudia said, "I remember how dusty the road was, and what it was like riding in back of the truck on our way to church because we didn't have a car." I remember those rides in the back of the truck fondly. It was an adventure riding back there. It's remarkable how different siblings' recollections can be, often because of age and gender.

Later, Claudia also sold furniture at Schneiderman's, both at the Meadowlands store and part-time at the Duluth location. She was good at it. Today, though she could retire, Claudia's involved in buying for a nice, higher-end boutique in Jackson

Hole, Wyoming. I'm not sure of all her responsibilities, but I know she attends markets and works on merchandising, among other things. She and her husband, Michael, love Jackson Hole and enjoy their grandchildren. Claudia's daughter, Jennifer, earned a PhD in pharmacology and a law degree and she's working as a patent attorney in the medical field. Claudia's son, Joel, is a lieutenant colonel in the U.S. Air Force.

The five younger Schneiderman children, despite many differences among us, share three characteristics: we know how to work, we know how to sell, and we have a core belief in God.

Many people stayed away from our store at first. Probably in part because we were strangers. People in small towns are very cliquish. Then there was how Joe Constanzi's murder spree had affected the whole town, but especially the families of the victims. So it was tough. While Dad had a lot of pride, he also had a sense of when he needed to just suck it up, knowing that in the long run it would be worth it.

Right after buying a new car, a neighbor asked my dad, "Do you want to take a ride with me? Do you want to drive?" Dad had never owned a new car. Looking back, I imagine Dad must have felt some jealousy. He didn't get his first new car until he was 57 years old: a red 1967 Ford Galaxy 500 XL.

"No, I'll ride with you," Dad told the neighbor.

They drove around the block. We called it a block, but really it was a two-mile drive. Unbeknownst to the driver, Dad was simmering the entire ride. Finally, when they got back to the store he said, "You know, I'm impressed that you could get a new car like this, but maybe you could pay me for the hot water heater you bought from me a year and a half ago."

The neighbor was pretty angry. His brother-in-law owned a large farm with several workers and may have been our best grocery customer—and he abruptly stopped shopping at our store. Just like that. In a small town, that's what happens.

The man told his brother-in-law that Dad was *dunning* him—harassing him over money owed. We don't use that word much anymore, but that's what he said. When the brother-in-law stopped coming to the store, my dad went out to talk to him, which must have been tough, because he had a lot of pride. He asked what we had done wrong. Why wasn't he buying from us anymore?

He said, "Well, you were dunning my brother-in-law."

So, my dad told him what had happened with the water heater. I remember Dad telling me the man turned red in the face and muttered something about my dad not being the first to get the shaft from the guy. He assured Dad he would start shopping with him again and he was good for his word.

In a rural area, everyone knows everyone, and in many cases people are related. If you tick off one of them, you tick off the whole family. That was one of the downsides of being in the grocery business in a small town. You have to cater to a limited group of people and it could be pretty unfair at times. Often in the summer, farmers would make hay late into the evening. When they were done, they'd often ring the doorbell and one of us would go down into the store and let them in to buy milk and bread. Often, they'd ask to charge it. This bothered Max because these same people would often buy their bulk groceries in the nearby towns of Hibbing or Duluth, but then wake my parents in the middle of the night for a bottle of milk.

Despite some of these common problems in a small town, my parents seemed to know exactly when to swallow a little pride and when to stand up for themselves. Later on, when our business moved exclusively to home furnishings, whenever we encountered problems, my parents always had an answer: "Hey, be thankful," they'd say. "You could be in the grocery business."

Dad and Mom both had excellent business sense. They always wanted to please their customers, accommodate requests, and were committed to getting people good prices. My dad made a lot of friends at Marshall-Wells because he had that kind of personality. When Marshall-Wells was going to close, Dad was particularly interested in their hardware stock. They had a huge hardware department, including building materials, windows, and tile. In their 1980s interview with freelance writer Jane Brissette, my parents talk about how they eventually got more customers coming to the store in the early 1950s.

> EDNA. Well, persistence I guess. We started fixing up the place, and people had to start coming to get their mail. Gradually they found us. They probably came in from curiosity at first, who knows. Then, they were just beginning to get electricity around here and they were beginning to modernize so we got pretty heavy into hardware. Well, we had electricity, but we didn't have any running water. We had a well, but people were beginning to put in bathrooms and so on. However, we did have the best stock of copper pipe and all that didn't we?

> MAX. Eventually.

> EDNA. Eventually; then just gradually we built it up through the hardware.

> MAX. At the time electrical was hard to get.

> EDNA. . . . After the war.

> MAX. And I was fortunate. I wanted an electric range, and an appliance wholesaler said he would give it to me, but when I went down to get it he turned me down. So, I went over to Marshall-Wells, the wholesaler I would use, and I was very, very, fortunate. They sent me to the guy who was in charge of all that stuff and he got me the electric range. He came up here one day a few months later to see how I was getting along when a customer came in with a big long list he wanted for

electrical. Evidently, he'd been shopping it. So, I said, "Well, I'd have to go down and find out what I can get for you." This guy from Marshall-Wells took the sheet and looked at it and said you can have it all. I got some lucky breaks.

EDNA. [*laughs*] You got a lot of lucky breaks! And after you'd built it all up really well, which was quite a few years later, Marshall-Wells went out of business. That's when you got another lucky break right?

MAX. Yeah, they sent a guy here from New York to close the place down. Somehow or another he had invited me out for coffee. So, I went up and had coffee with him. After that, he [left] a note for when I came in [that] said he would like to talk to me. They had decided to close and he offered 10 percent under the wholesale price for dealers. I sat there, and like a dope, I said to the guy, "You know some big shot is going to come in here. They're going to want to buy all this stuff and you're not going to give them just 10 percent, you're going to want to give them more than that." I'll never forget that conversation, but he looked at me and he said, "How does 20 percent sound?" So I said, "Fine." At the time I knew a fellow who worked at First American Bank. I knew him fairly well. I told him I had this opportunity and I wanted to know how much money could I draw. He said, "As far as you want to go." And I really went.

EDNA. That was several years after you'd been here and you had established your credit. They felt Max could be trusted. They really did go overboard on that, but it gave us a great big boost. We were able to sell so many things way below what anybody could even touch. It kind of made our reputation.

Mom always insisted that one of the most important truths in business was that good credit was better than money in the bank.

At the time, I'm sure Mr. Craig, the New Yorker sent to close out Marshall-Wells, thought of my dad as a small-time store owner. He didn't realize Dad was a big thinker and a big gambler. As Dad told the story, he already had 15 truckloads moved from Marshall-Wells to our Elmer store before Mr. Craig had heard of what was going on and approached him.

He said, "You know, Max, I think you've gotten enough now." Dad stopped, but by that time, he had more than enough. My dad thought big and knew this investment would pay off.

So now he had large amounts of corrugated tin roofing, windows, rubber tile, cast-iron pipe, and electrical supplies that he ended up buying at 10 to 20 cents on the dollar. Dad bought so much we didn't have enough space to store it all inside. A large portion of the construction supplies had to be stored outside. Dad would sell the stuff at a wholesale price to people so they got a good deal. After the war, people began adding bathrooms, running water, and electricity to their homes. Dad could get his customers what they needed, and cheaper than they could buy it anywhere else. This may well have been the basis for Dad's strong belief in word-of-mouth advertising. People from the Iron Range as well as Duluth and other surrounding communities began hearing about this little store that had an impressive inventory and low prices on hard-to-get building materials.

The building materials were part of a pattern of leveraging the business to buy more stock. He started with the original grocery store and then he built on the larger grocery store. It was kind of a big deal. We had a huge grand opening with drawings for baskets of groceries and other prizes, including a premium mattress and box spring. Dad had a flare for promotions, even within a small town.

After the grand opening of the larger grocery store, Dad put a few pieces of furniture in the older part of the store. Eventually, a banker named Bob Maly loaned my father the money to build a great big furniture store onto the grocery store. There was no logical way to justify the loan, except that my dad always paid back everything he borrowed and Maly had faith in him. It was crazy, really—a big furniture store in a town in the middle of nowhere. Even calling Elmer a town seems like an exaggeration.

According to Mom:

> Max was gone a whole lot and I would have to take over the whole place because he would go to get things from Duluth all the time. It was so lucky; it was just the time rural homeowners were putting in electricity. We didn't have [what they needed] at first. Then they put in kitchens, bathrooms, and stuff. It was a perfect time for somebody with a lot of energy, and my gosh! Max had a lot of energy. He'd come home with that truck loaded with stuff and I would say, "Oh, my heaven's sakes!" It was perfectly okay as long as he met his bills, and he always paid his bills and had good credit all over, at the bank or wherever.

The grocery business remained important initially, but word of mouth started to spread about the furniture store. The grocery and hardware store remained until I graduated from high school in 1967. We all worked in the grocery store doing one thing or another. Finally, in 1968 my parents got out of groceries and hardware and focused on furniture, appliances, and carpeting.

The whole time Dad was buying and buying. He would buy nearly any bargain he could get his hands on. Sometimes he went overboard on a good deal—for example, galvanized aluminum buckets. We had thousands of them, all over the place. Then he bought dozens of sewing machines. I don't know what made him think he was going to get rid of all of them, but he did.

Maybe the best bulk-bargain purchase he made was when we painted the entire exterior of the store pink. Pink of all colors! I asked Dad why he chose that color: "Because I got a deal on *that* color paint."

That's the way he was. It was the way he thought, and it was one of the characteristics that made him a great businessman.

His bold and often unexpected choices were the beginning of the Schneiderman's stores as they exist today.

One of my father's favorite sayings was, "There's only two things wrong with the furniture business. That is employees and customers." So it was with reluctance that Dad hired help outside the family. He hired a part-time salesman, but he didn't work out. He also hired local men to help him deliver furniture. During Christmas break from college, I delivered furniture with one of those men. He showed up carrying the biggest thermos you could ever imagine. He would sip coffee all day long and the first thing he'd say when we got to a customer's house was, "Do you have a bathroom?"

"I don't know, stuff just goes right through me," he'd tell me.

Another guy I delivered with enjoyed stopping at a tavern on the way home from deliveries. So, there I was, underage and drinking beer with him at Kacer's in Kelsey—the Airport Store outside Hibbing—and other bars. At that age I wasn't concerned about our "brand" when our Schneiderman's truck was sitting out in front of the bar.

Our first non-family employee of substance was Clyde Morse. Clyde graduated from high school in 1963, the same year as my sister Claudia. Clyde was your typical farm boy. He was one of those people who had the ability to figure out anything, who was strong as could be and trustworthy. Clyde became our all-purpose guy, and part of the family in a way. He was in charge of the warehouse and furniture repair, as well as making extra deliveries. He was like a son to my mom and dad, and he viewed them like family, too. I guess he was like a brother to me because he was in my wedding party.

In 1963, my mom and dad took their first vacation—to Jamaica—on a free trip given away by a mattress or carpet company. The companies we buy from don't do this anymore because of the pressure to get lower pricing on things, but at the time, if a dealer reached a predetermined quota, he would earn an all-expenses-paid trip. My parents never would have gone on a vacation if they had to pay for it themselves. After that first trip, they went on a vacation nearly every year for over 20 years. Mom especially loved travel and learning about new places. They traveled nearly the entire world by the time they were done. We all had opportunities to go on some of these trips with them. To this day, Sheila and I recall our visit to Holland with Mom, Dad, Karen, and Bob as maybe the best trip we've ever been on.

While Mom and Dad were away, my sisters, my brothers-in-law, and my brother Phil would handle the business. By that time, we were starting to get busy on the weekends so Clyde was brought in to help on the sales floor. That's when we received a pleasant surprise—Clyde could sell! When Russ and I eventually bought the business, Clyde became our warehouse manager. When the store was busy, we'd ask him to come inside to help us sell and he'd always do a good job. As the warehouse manager, he was still a one-man-band. Eventually, we hired a couple people to help him in the warehouse, but Clyde couldn't stand being a manager, being responsible for the warehouse employees. If Clyde wanted something done, he would just do it. He said if he had to remain the warehouse manager, he'd have to quit because he couldn't stand it. So, I offered him the chance to be a full-time salesperson. He took the job because it was better than managing people. Customers loved him and he taught me an important lesson about what it takes to be a successful furniture salesman: Selling furniture isn't about being slick and trying to get someone to buy something they don't want. Being a salesperson is showing that you're honest and have the knowledge and the ability to follow through. And it doesn't hurt to know a little bit about interior decorating.

People loved Clyde, and he became an excellent addition to the extended Schneiderman family. Clyde worked for us for over 42 years. He was a good worker, no matter what he did, farmer, salesman, or warehouse manager (as long as he didn't have to manage people). Even though Clyde was in our smaller Meadowlands store, he was always one of the top sales consultants in the entire company. When working with customers, there wasn't a rock Clyde wouldn't upturn to help them find exactly what they wanted. A couple of years after he retired, I asked him if he wanted to come and help us with the Meadowlands closing sale. He did, even though it was painful; after over 42 years in the warehouse and on the sales floor, he'd developed knee problems.

Schneiderman's has been something of a family affair for Clyde's family as well. His wife, June, still works at the company, for more than 36 years as of 2013. Our customer care and administrative offices remain in Meadowlands and we have a number of long-term, dedicated people, but June stands out in my mind. At one time June's mother, Aileen, helped us with the housekeeping. I called her Sunshine, because of her wonderful, sunny disposition. June's sister, Donna, was an excellent administrative assistant, and at one time, June's brother-in-law worked for us. In May 2013, June's daughter-in-law, Nicole Morse, became the Financial Manager.

This is just one example of the loyalty we have with the long line of associates and their families. This commitment to each other bolsters the foundation of our company.

And the whole family's connection to Schneiderman's started with Clyde.

5

Second Generation

By 1965, in my teens, I was already excited about the furniture business and I loved to sell. Dad incorporated the store in 1968, when I was 19 years old. My mother owned 25 percent, my Dad owned 25 percent, and the five children, all of us except David, each owned 10 percent. After our college graduation in 1971, some of my friends got jobs at big department stores as managers and I was happy for them, but I had no interest in those stores whatsoever. Mom and Dad were doing well in the business. I liked living in Meadowlands and I saw a lot of room for growth. The retail furniture business was a challenge I wanted to take on, and Dad knew I'd be good at it.

After I started working full time in the store, I started to realize more and more how much of a passion the store was becoming for me. It was more than just a job in the family business. I began to think in terms of expansion—even opening additional locations. I wasn't content to operate the business the same way my parents had operated it. I visited furniture stores in the Twin Cities every chance I got, and tried to initiate changes at our store. It wasn't long before it was apparent that my opinions were different from other family members who were active in the store, which caused some tensions among us.

Adding to my concerns about shared ownership of the store, a good friend of mine who owned part of a fine women's apparel business almost lost his business due to his parents' lack of sound financial planning. Because Dad hated having anything to do with lawyers, I asked him to meet with our business insurance agent, Michael Abramson, about estate planning. After listening to Mike and me, he responded, "You're like a couple of goddamned vultures up on a telephone wire, waiting for me to die."

In 1973, I tried again to talk to Dad about buying his and Mom's shares. I remember him telling me, "You know what? If you don't leave me alone, I'm not going to play cards with you anymore." We used to play Smear together while we talked about the store.

I knew it was an empty threat, but I finally got to the point where I told him, "You know, Dad, you're not doing anything about this and I can understand why. But I'm not going to work here, build this thing up, and then ultimately not own the business and be able to make decisions."

I wanted to own the business and have the freedom to make decisions about it. By this time, I enjoyed a solid friendship and business relationship with Jerry Jubie, who was the primary owner of the bank in nearby Floodwood. He assured me a loan would be no problem.

I offered both of my parents a sum of money to sell their shares to me. My mother was all for it. She wanted to see something done about the future of the business. My father said, "The only way I'll do it is if you buy your mother's shares and your brother Russell buys my shares so you're in business with him."

I told them I could live with that. I think they were concerned about what Russ was going to do if he worked at the store and I ended up taking over. Or perhaps Dad thought I wouldn't agree to that, so the process would be prolonged further. Russ was working in our warehouse at the time. He and I were close already and I figured we'd get along well running the business. So that's what we did and it all became official on September 15, 1979.

My older brother Phil, who mentored me in a lot of ways, soon approached me. Chemical dependency and gambling meant he needed money frequently. "Minority shares aren't going to help me and I don't see myself ever wanting to be in the business here. What would you give me for my shares?" So Phil was the first to sell. Then Claudia, who had little interest in the business at the time, heard Phil had gotten money for his shares and she approached me. We told her what we'd given Phil and offered her the same. She said that was fine.

My oldest sister, Karen, was a different story. Bob, her husband, was still working for Schneiderman's at that time. Despite having her own design business, she wasn't interested in selling her shares. We didn't approach her and she didn't approach us. Years later, she decided the shares weren't doing her much good and Russ and I purchased them.

Ultimately, Russ and I each wound up with 50 percent of the corporation. In time, we gifted shares to Russell's two children, Molly and John, twins who are the same age as my daughter Jenna. They have both graduated from college and have promising careers in business. My three children—Jason, Jodi, and Jenna—were also gifted shares. When Russ passed away on August 10, 2011, we had a buy/sell agreement funded by insurance already in place.

Once Dad sold the business to us, he decided he didn't want to work at the store. In fact, he made it clear he didn't want any responsibilities—and quickly. Soon Dad turned over financial matters to me. Shortly after that, he announced, "Larry is better at customer problems, take them to him." I have fond memories of working with Dad. We got along well and often had a lot of fun and laughed a lot. So, as he phased himself from the business, I missed being able to bounce things off him. I had envisioned he would transition slowly into retirement, but would still be around the store every day. But he knew I loved the business and I think stepping away was his way of supporting and encouraging this new phase of Schneiderman's Furniture. Even before I came to work at the store full time, Dad would tell people, "When Larry graduates from college he is going to take over the business." That had finally come to pass, in partnership with Russ, despite Dad's initial resistance. He built up the business and now he was ready to pass the store along to the next generation. I think another factor in his choice to step aside was that as the store grew, I noticed Dad had become more and more frustrated about issues with employees and customers—those were challenges he didn't enjoy.

Looking back, Dad's expectation of me was somewhat unfortunate because I had two older brothers-in-law who were working at the store. I didn't think about it then, but now I wonder what they must have thought. They were working there, putting up with my dad, and I was going to come in and be their boss. Another thing I didn't really think about at the time was that, in reality, my sisters would have never been given a chance to run the business. In Dad's mind, I was going to take over his legacy.

My style is more formal than Dad's was, and after he retired he'd have some fun at my expense from time to time. For example, he'd be mowing his lawn with his shirt off and then would drop into the store and sit down with a customer. He could barely hold back his laughter as he watched me squirm a little.

One of my new responsibilities after college graduation was to do the buying. Some of the factory representatives who called on me had been around a long time. One older guy, who was one of those people who feels certain he knows everything, represented a high-quality line of furniture called National Mount Airy. They made fine bedroom and dining room furniture in North Carolina, but have long since gone out of business. Unfortunately, their line didn't sell well for us. Twice a year, the rep had specials for 10 percent off the wholesale price. He'd start in with his slick sales pitch. He called my dad "Maxy," something no one called him.

"Maxy always bought bedroom and dining room furniture at 10 percent off," the rep told me.

I said, "We don't need any more of your bedroom furniture. We have plenty in the warehouse. But I will fill in the dining room."

"You're not going to buy the bedroom?"

"No, we don't need it."

He said, "Well, Maxy always bought the bedroom."

I politely replied, "Well, we don't need it." What I didn't tell him is I knew he had a spell over my dad and we always had too much Mount Airy inventory. My dad couldn't say no to him. The rep wrote up the dining room sale and we said goodbye. About half an hour later, I received a call from my dad.

"Larry, what are you doing?" he asked. It was his standard opening.

"Working," I said. It was my standard reply.

"Can you come over here for a little bit?" he asked.

"Sure."

My parents had a house right around the corner from the store. I went over and I saw this Mount Airy sales rep's car over by the garage and I was thinking, "Oh, man." I went in the house and my dad told the rep, "Tell Larry what you told me."

I could see he was nervous. "Larry, I said you seem like a smart young man and you're probably going to do well in this business, but you have some things to learn."

Then my dad prompted, "Well. Like what?"

"Well, like for instance, you didn't take advantage of the bedroom discount and I think that's a big mistake on your part."

I was really getting upset by then, so I asked, "You didn't like that I didn't order the bedroom so you came over here to complain about it to my dad?"

"Well, no, no. I wanted to get together with Maxy and say hello, and yeah, it just came up."

"Okay, the order for the dining room furniture. Tear it up. Cancel it," I told him. "See you later, Dad," I said as I walked away. After I got back to the store and received another call from my dad. He said, "What are you doing?"

"Working."

"Can you come over here?"

"Is he gone?" I asked.

"Yeah, he's gone."

When I went back over to the house Dad said, "You know what? I'm glad you did that. I've always hated that son of a bitch."

I remember I wasn't particularly concerned with my dad affirming the decision, because I knew it was the right one. But it was an interesting lesson to see how the Mount Airy rep perceived my dad was his buddy, while my dad, for whatever reason, allowed himself to be pressured into ordering stuff he didn't want.

Dad was extremely loyal to people who treated him well. We were a small furniture dealer at the time. My parents carried the Flexsteel line from the beginning of their furniture business; today Flexsteel is our leading vendor in dollars. Jack Crahan was the president of Flexsteel in those days. The company would fly retailers to their plant in Dubuque, Iowa, in their corporate jet and show them their new products and offer tours of the plant. My dad, always on the lookout for money-saving ideas, got himself and Mom invited to the plant. He planned to rent a car there and then drive to see my sister, Karen, who was living in Dixon, Illinois, about 100 miles from Dubuque. When Dad told Crahan his plans, he took a set of keys from his pocket, gave them to Dad, and said, "Here, take my car." This isn't the only instance of my dad's loyalty reflecting back to him. He had many of these good-begets-good relationships.

Another example of Dad's encouragement during my early days running the company came when an acquaintance offered up an odd comment. We did a lot of business with a great family who owned a manufacturing business near Duluth. They built homes and would recommend our store to their clients and, in turn, we'd send our customers to them. As with our store, the next generation was starting to get involved in running their business. One brother of the family was a little eccentric. We didn't have a bad relationship—it was somewhat neutral, I guess. He was in our store one Sunday when, without prompting, he said, "You know, Larry, no matter how successful you may be, you won't be half the businessman your dad is."

I remember wondering why he was telling me that. "I agree with you," I said. In my heart, I didn't exactly agree with him, but I had tremendous respect for my dad. I wasn't going to argue.

I was playing cards with my dad a little later—Smear, of course. We'd talk back and forth while we were playing. I told him what the guy had said to me earlier.

"Larry, who you are got you where you are. Who you need to be will get you the rest of the way." I liked that idea.

Dad's pride in what Russ and I accomplished was obvious. Duluth was our first expansion, and then we opened up the first Lakeville store in 1984. Dad teased, "Larry, you'll sell more furniture than I ever sold, but you'll never make the money I did." He turned out to be a prophet on that one. He had a strong intuition that the small business with a hands-on entrepreneur is a superior model to depending on a lot of other people to operate your business. Dad knew about the dangers of expansion. It's a double-edged sword. Do you attempt to keep things as they are and nurture your present business? Or do you expand, knowing that will create more challenges, but possibly greater rewards? The wrong answer to this question has been the cause of countless business failures—and countless family-business controversies. At this point, Russ and I didn't put a lot of energy into thinking about it, but we loved discussing and thinking about expansion.

By 1987 Russ was living in the Twin Cities with his family, and Schneiderman's had opened a store in Minnetonka that he managed. Dad's health was already declining by then, but as we talked about the expansion he said, "If I was young, it is exactly what I would do." He was extremely encouraging about what we were doing.

Mom, by contrast, was always concerned about our health— our mental well-being. Whenever we'd take on a new business challenge, she'd say, "Ah! You're going to have so much to worry about and to think about. Are you sure you want to do that?"

Russ and I were close from the beginning. He was fond of saying, "Larry and I have never had an argument since we've been partners." Well, one of the things we agreed on is we would never make a business move that would jeopardize the business itself. If we thought the worst-case scenario could put us out of business, we wouldn't do it. Obviously, in order to grow as we did, we both had to be interested in the growth or it wouldn't have worked.

It was Russ's wife who pushed him to grow further in the company and become more involved. Initially Russ was working in the warehouse in Meadowlands and seemed content to keep working there. Then he married Monica, who asked him, "You're a Schneiderman. What are you doing working in the warehouse?"

He came and talked to me about it and surprised me a little by asking, "Do you think I could learn how to sell?"

I didn't doubt Russ could sell and he turned out to be a phenomenal salesman. In all the roles I saw him take on, selling was his greatest strength. Even when he was no longer regularly on the sales floor in Lakeville, he would still assist certain customers. He was a great salesman. Even in his last working years, after making a nice sale, he would stop by my office and flip the big sales order in front of me. We never tired of our little inside jokes.

My parents built their furniture business in Elmer without ever having a formal sale or, more importantly, without advertising. While I wasn't there to see this, my dad loved to tell this story.

There was a gathering of a large number of Sealy mattress retailers in Minneapolis. They had invited Dad to take part because Schneiderman's was a good Sealy customer. The moderator of the program made a point of saying, "As good retailers, your goal should be to sell higher-end mattresses and better beds instead of cheap beds." According to Sealy, the retailer selling the highest percentage of premium mattresses was Schneiderman's, up in the sticks between Hibbing and Duluth in a little town called Meadowlands. The moderator invited my dad to stand and asked if anyone had any questions for him. One attendee commented, "In order to do that, you must spend a tremendous amount of money advertising."

I can just picture the moment. Dad would get this look on his face when he was about to impart a pearl of wisdom. I knew that look well. He took off his glasses, as if reflecting on the question, and said, "Well, I do take an ad out in the local school's yearbook."

After there was some low murmuring, and another guy asked, "Well, what other advertising do you do?" But the yearbook was it; he just didn't spend money for advertising. And his model worked: a single-price, nonnegotiable, and low mark-up business.

Dad had a firm core of business beliefs. They were his three pillars: 1.) Don't spend money on advertising when word-of-mouth advertising is free. 2.) No sales. 3.) Commission selling is a bad thing. Those pillars worked well—for him.

Dad told me more than once that it's helpful that things go wrong sometimes, because it gives you the opportunity to show new customers your word is good, to prove you're worthy of their trust. Those moments are a kind of word-of-mouth advertising. Russ and I experienced this firsthand when an understandably upset customer came in. She had bought a nice bedroom set with a premium king-size mattress. Our warehouse had sent a queen-size mattress in error. When our drivers got there and the mistake was discovered, our driver said we would exchange the pieces on Tuesday. It was a Friday and the customer called the store around 5:00 p.m., which was when we closed. I happened to take the call. "Either you bring my mattress tonight," the customer said, "or we'll go to a store here in Duluth and pick up a new one."

I assured them we would get it to them. I called Russ, who said he wasn't doing anything. So the two of us loaded the truck with the correct items and headed for Duluth. As we assembled the frame, the customer asked Russ, "What kind of people are the Schneidermans?"

Russ deadpanned, "They're the best. I wouldn't want to work for anybody else."

The customer commented, "I've heard the same thing. It's nice to hear an employee say that."

When the business started growing larger, and our family members could no longer do all the selling, Russ and I decided an incentive system was needed. So we introduced sales commissions.

Dad was already retired by then, so I don't know how he heard about the decision. I hadn't discussed it with him. Anyway, he was so upset when he heard about the commissions that he walked around the corner from their house to the store. He came into my office and shut the door. He wanted to know "what the hell" was going on—was it true that we were paying commissions?

"Yeah, it's true," I told him, expecting him to be okay with it.

Instead, he stuck his index finger in my face and said, "The reason this place was successful is because we didn't have any commissions. Commissions make people pushy."

"Well, Dad, I respectfully disagree. You and Mother were the ultimate commission sales consultants. If you didn't sell, you didn't eat. You had that kind of incentive." I pointed to a woman nearby, Sharon, who was one of our sales consultants. "She doesn't have that kind of incentive, and she needs something to reward her for her extra efforts."

"I think you need to get rid of paying commissions right now. Not having them was one of the reasons we were successful."

"The salespeople are excited about it. We're implementing commissions, and they're going to stay."

But it didn't matter what I said, he was already mad at me. His reaction to me, or anybody, when he got upset was the silent treatment. And I got a dose of it for a couple weeks or so until we got together to play Smear again.

In the current commission system, our sales consultants receive a monthly draw. It's above the minimum wage, but it's not a livable wage. In the past, it seemed as if more people preferred the commission system because if you work hard, you're rewarded. More and more, though, we're finding that people—especially our younger salespeople—don't like the idea of depending on their sales for income. It's one of the reasons we sometimes discuss moving away from the system. However, we only know of two successful furniture businesses that don't use commissions, and even those examples figure some incentives into the mix.

In my view, people should be rewarded if they have more ability, work harder, and out-perform the others. Let's face it, in any group there will be somebody on the top and somebody on the bottom. At one of our locations, we have 26 sales consultants total. There's always a top seller and a seller coming in 26th. We have sales minimums, so managers tend to spend a disproportionate amount of time trying to bring the bottom people up. This doesn't serve the company well because if the managers' time was spent with the top performers, they would be more likely to grow their sales than the lower-tier folks would. Currently, our top performer, in addition to working her 42-hour schedule, including almost all weekends, makes house calls on her day off. Would she do that if she were being paid the same as everyone else? I don't know why she would.

In addition to posing hiring challenges, another disadvantage with the commission system is that it is very difficult to foster a team approach. The sales people are in business for themselves. One practice of the system is that sales consultants work off an opportunity sheet. The first person arriving in the morning will tend to the first customer, and so on. They get a little competitive about who is "their" customer. They often don't see a customer as a Schneiderman's customer; they see the person as their customer. For the most part, they get along with each other, but a sales consultant who is too ambitious can cause waves. Sometimes we'll hire a new person who turns out to be phenomenal. Some of the experienced sales consultants can pressure the new person, which can hurt the sales consultant and the store, and it doesn't serve the customer.

We want our sales consultants to be walking through the store all the time. If a customer needs help, we need to be available, and make sure the customer knows people are around to help. Sometimes, though, if a customer is assigned to a particular consultant, the others try to avoid contact with that customer at all. They don't even smile at the customer, for fear they'll ask for help. So it appears the sales consultant is being unfriendly.

There are pros and cons for both commission and salary-only systems, but I think the benefits outweigh the drawbacks with the commission system. My son, Jason, and I sometimes discuss trying a different type of system, commission, salary, or a combination of both, but it would be a big deal. Changes to employee pay structures create anxiety and uncertainty, sometimes even bitterness. It's doubtful we could test out a change and then "rewind" if the results were poor. We have a large number of sales consultants who do well on commission, and it seems the best option at present.

We post our customers' Bill of Rights at every one of our locations. We don't have them because they sound nice—we refer to them quite often. It outlines what we need to do and what we expect. We use the same form as the employees' Bill of Rights. Basically, you need to treat each other like you would treat the customers. There are businesses that sell a lot more furniture than Schneiderman's and businesses that make a lot more money—but I don't think, based on the evidence I've seen, there is a better bunch of people in terms of how they treat people. Vendors often tell me that Schneiderman's is their favorite account.

Several years ago, I was walking down an aisle at the High Point Market, a large home furnishings trade show held in North Carolina. I noticed a young lady straining to read my name badge. She approached me and said, "I have always said if I ever meet the owner of Schneiderman's, I am going to give him a big hug. Your company is my favorite!" And she gave me a hug.

6

Phil's Struggles

Before my brother Phil's memorial service in Duluth, three of his friends called me and asked if they could say something at the service. "Of course! That's great, that's great!" I told them.

All three of them knew Phil at the University of Minnesota and each told a variation on the same theme: Phil was the smartest person they'd ever met. One friend talked about how he was struggling in a math course, and knew he was going to fail the final exam. So he asked Phil, who hadn't taken the course, if he could take the exam for him. Phil got a B. Recently I was reminiscing about that story with Phil's friend and he said Phil told him he could've gotten an A, but he didn't want to arouse suspicion.

To my knowledge, Phil is the only person to skip a grade at Toivola-Meadowlands. He was in first grade, and when the kids were in a circle learning to read, he would turn his book upside down and read it. He had taught himself to read.

Intellectually, Phil was on top of it. In other ways, he was not. He threw away a lot of money. As a young man, he got a high-paying job as a store manager at United Furniture, a big furniture store in Minneapolis. Later he received his trading license and was a stockbroker. (At one point, the Securities and Exchange Commission asked Phil to avoid further involvement in trading. That's all I know about it. Phil and I never spoke about it.) He was involved in several partnerships and ultimately owned part of Livon Manufacturing, a company specializing in quality living room furniture. At times in his life, he had a lot of money, but the same things always tripped him up—drinking and gambling.

Phil and my dad had a volatile relationship when he was growing up. I remember, and Russ did too, terrible fights between them. Phil was like a man-child. He was unbelievably strong and a tremendous football player. He was actually an all-state player. He worked hard at it. However, he had a habit my dad would not tolerate in people—lying. Phil would lie.

My dad had, to his own and others' misfortune, an inability to forget or forgive certain things people did. One of those unforgivable events occurred at our grocery store. Phil, as an eighth grader, served as the student manager of the basketball team. Phil was caught by my dad stealing cigarettes for the players on the team. If Dad told me the story once, he told me 50 times. It was his go-to example of Phil's biggest flaw, his need to be a big shot. My dad was a humble person and he hated to see arrogance in people.

Phil had a curfew and consistently ignored it, even if that meant screaming fights when he got home. They argued a lot. One time, Phil fell asleep at the wheel on his way home and put the car in a ditch. He said he swerved to avoid a deer. It caused considerable damage to the vehicle. He and Dad went back to the scene early the next morning and there were no deer tracks. My dad was beyond angry about the lie. I can't help but wonder if incidents like that one were early glimpses of his alcoholism.

I don't know for sure *when* Phil began to drink, although I'm guessing it was early. I know some of the arguments my father and Phil had while he was in high school were about his drinking. Drinking among high-school students was not uncommon in northern Minnesota in the 1950s and '60s.

After high school, Phil moved out of the house and enrolled at the University of Minnesota in St. Paul and my parents were paying his tuition. I don't know how it eventually surfaced, but they found out that instead of attending classes he was playing cards. Dad was livid. That was the end of Phil's college education and he remained 16 credits short of attaining a degree.

Phil loved the furniture business. He was a sales consultant at our Lakeville store when we opened in 1984. Then a personal incident occurred that led to Phil's resignation. Years later he became the store manager for the Schneiderman's in Meadowlands. While he held that position in the family company, he also became the sales manager of a furniture manufacturing company we started, American Furniture Craftsmen. Phil was highly skilled and knowledgeable about manufacturing processes, which I know because we spent many hours discussing manufacturing processes. We had our own private book club as we studied the various theories. I asked him to oversee the plant.

Then it started.

Phil couldn't just drink a little. He was the classic, bottle-of-vodka-during-the-day alcoholic. He wound up in detox and was supposed to go to Alcoholics Anonymous (AA). One of the things we discovered later about Phil was that he never felt AA was where he belonged. He felt he had nothing in common with these people; but of course, he had everything in common with them. He was so intelligent, but could never get past his addictions. He couldn't get past Step 1, admitting powerlessness over alcohol.

When Phil was calling on a good account for American Furniture Craftsmen, I had one of my more disastrous professional experiences with him. Before they closed their doors in 2008 as a result of the recession, Kacey Furniture was a strong second-generation, Denver-based operation. At the time of the incident, they were an important account. Phil had an appointment in Denver with the owners. When they asked where he was staying, he said he needed to get a hotel room. "You're not staying in a hotel," they told him. "You're going to stay with us." He stayed with them, got drunk, and revealed some important information about one of our vendors who was giving us advertising money.

Soon after, I got a call at my office in Meadowlands from the national sales manager of this major vendor. "What's going on? I got a call from Leslie at Kacey's and she was extremely upset. Somehow she knew how much advertising money you're getting. Larry, they're a bigger account than you are and you're getting more money."

I apologized, of course. I had a strong suspicion about what had happened.

Then I got a call from Leslie Fishbein, the owner of Kacey's. She was angry and wanted me to confirm what Phillip had let slip. I told her I wouldn't confirm the amount of advertising money Schneiderman's was receiving because it was confidential. The incident, unfortunately, ended our positive relationship with Kacey's.

When Phil returned, I could hardly wait to see him. He was bigger than me and stronger—an intimidating guy who could push his weight around if he chose to do so. But that day I think I could have wrung his neck. "You got drunk didn't you?" I asked.

"No!" he claimed. "What I'm trying to do is assemble a group of good retailers to get more of what we're entitled to.

Thanks a lot, Larry. Here I am trying to do this—"

"Phil, I know the best defense is a strong offense, but you're being ridiculous," I interrupted. "You know that's confidential information. I'm telling you now, you've made your last trip for me. I can't trust you." It was the last sales trip he made for American Furniture Craftsmen.

Then Phil wound up having another incident. He lived in an apartment in Alborn, a town about 20 minutes from Meadowlands. I got a call from somebody living near him, who told me I'd better get over there right away. It was May, but it was still cold, and there was snow on the ground. He was out on the street with bare feet and no shirt, yelling at cars as they went by. I called 911 and went with him to the detox center. I knew the EMT who rode in the back with us. All the way to the center, Phil kept saying how much he loved me. Now I realize how tragic it all was. Then, I admit, I was embarrassed.

Phil struck again. I told him, "This can't happen again. This makes two strikes. Third strike, you're out."

"I understand, I understand."

"What are you going to do so it doesn't happen again?"

"I need to take my drinking problem seriously."

Phil decided to meet with a psychiatrist and allowed the doctor to speak with me directly about his treatment. For the first time in a long time, I thought Phil had made a good decision regarding his recovery. By giving his permission for the doctor to speak to me, and allowing me to make decisions on his behalf, Phil was starting to demonstrate that he really wanted to get help for himself. A few days later, I was in my office when I got a call from a salesperson in the Meadowlands store. He said I should come over right away. I went over and Phil was in his office with a big cut on his head. He was reeking of booze and slurring.

"What happened to your head?"

"I fell," he told me. "I was getting out of my apartment and there was an icy spot and I fell."

"Well, Phil, you smell like you've been drinking and you're slurring."

As was his habit when he was drinking, he got out of his chair and started yelling and swearing at me. Every other word was the F-enheimer. The sales consultants were nearby and heard all of it. "Phil, I didn't say you've been drinking. I said you smell and sound like you've been drinking. That means customers will think you've been drinking. I need you to go home."

He took off, still swearing, out to his car in the parking lot. About an hour and a half later I got a call from him, "Thank you for caring," he said sarcastically.

"What do you mean?" I asked.

"I'm in the emergency room. I got a concussion from when I fell. You know that's why I was slurring. The medications I take give me bad breath."

I said, "Well, stay right there and I'll come pick you up."

"No, no, they said it's okay for me to drive."

So I called St. Luke's emergency room. No Schneiderman. I called St. Mary's. No Schneiderman. I called Miller-Dwan. No Schneiderman. Then I called Phil's counselor and he gave me some advice I'll never forget. Many times over the years, I've encountered employees and others with chemical dependency issues, and I've kept his words in mind.

"You know, Larry," he said. "The problem is that you don't understand that to an alcoholic, lying is like breathing. You *know* he's not in any of those emergency rooms. Why are you even telling me this? What is he going to say? Is he going to say, 'Yes, I've been drinking and I know you're going to fire me?' He doesn't have a choice but to lie to save his own skin. It's what alcoholics do."

Well, that episode was strike three and I told Phil, "You're done. I can't have it anymore. I can't trust you. You know I love you and I want you to get the help you need, but I can't have you working here."

There was some conflict within the family about my decision. My mother said, "You know you need to give your brother Phil another chance."

"I won't do it," I insisted. "He's had at least three chances, probably more. I won't do it."

Phil heard Mom was upset and went over to tell her, "It's not Larry's fault. It's my fault." I'm grateful that he did that, and I'll never forget it.

Phil was a tremendous motivator. I knew when I fired him it wouldn't necessarily be good for the business. He was a great idea person—very creative.

He could state his thoughts in truly memorable ways. Once in a company-wide store managers' meeting, we were talking about things sales consultants do to get us in trouble. Phil chimed in with, "My sales consultants keep shooting themselves in the foot, but that's okay. I can tell what they're doing by how they limp."

In all my years in business, I've never met anyone who was better at problem solving. "Any problem can be solved if you break it into little pieces and solve those," he told me once. The other thing he would focus on was finding the cause of a problem, not just treating its symptoms. While he was so talented at resolving problems at work, it was tragic he couldn't get to the root and solve his own problems.

As much as I like and understand the furniture business, he was way beyond me in problem-solving abilities and native intelligence. Soon after the day I fired him, right up until the time he died, he was often my Saturday-morning call. We'd talk. He wanted to know everything about the business. He ended up working for a number of furniture stores, at least a half dozen, throughout his career. Some of those situations had a similar end—fired because of his drinking. He had some other characteristics that made him difficult to get along with, beyond his struggle with addiction.

Sometimes Phil was a tough guy to work with and a tough guy to be around. He was so passionate about things and so persuasive about his point of view that he would wear you down. As his brother, I had lived with Phil's obsessions for years, but other people didn't have to accept his aggressive nature and it would get him in trouble occasionally.

At one point Phil was working for a furniture store in Florida and going through sales training. Remember, he was a guy who knew everything about furniture, plus he had no patience. I can just hear him over the phone, "And the goddamn trainer is this 23-year-old woman who doesn't know shit."

"Phil, are you even going to make it through training?" I was joking and at the same time, I wasn't. I could picture what was going to happen.

One time, Phil and I were flying to the furniture market and he didn't have his driver's license. The airline's customer service person asked for his identification. He said he didn't have any on him, and the woman told him he couldn't get a boarding pass without a driver's license. "I can't board?" Phil asked. "Do I look like a goddamn terrorist? I'm on my way to the furniture market!"

The customer service person called her manager immediately because Phil was menacing. He ended up contacting his roommate, who went to their house, made a copy of his license, and faxed it to the manager. We even made the plane on time. He could get his way through intimidation, and he often did.

The joke in our family was that Phil married three times and every time the woman had the same name, "Plaintiff." Carol was his first wife. She was very traditional. We liked her, everyone in the family did. They married in 1965 and had a son, Greg, in 1966. He was a great kid, and extremely good looking. Carol found Phil difficult to live with, and they divorced in 1975.

Greg was gay and his death from AIDS on January 6, 1994, had a serious long-term effect on Phil and his view on life. It was wrenching to watch Phil struggle with Greg's death. While most of the people in our family don't cry easily, Phil would often break down emotionally when the subject of Greg surfaced. He sometimes attributed his drinking problems to his sorrow.

About six months after his divorce from Carol, Phil married Liz, a woman with roots in New York. She was attractive and outgoing. I'm sure Phil's drinking put a strain on the marriage, though I don't know many details. Ultimately, they divorced also, and then remarried. Phil adopted Liz's son, Marc, from a previous marriage. I don't know how long Liz and Phil were married, but I think they had a civil relationship after the divorce.

My dad could have a ribald sense of humor, and Liz was an attractive girl. Prior to their marriage, Phil brought Liz home and they stayed with my mom and dad for a couple days. My mom planned for them to be in separate bedrooms, even though they were living together. When they got there, Phil said, "Mom, that's ridiculous. We live together."

"Well, what you do on your own is your business, but what you do in my house is my business."

Phil pleaded, "Dad, what are you thinking?"

"If I can watch, it's okay," Dad replied.

I think my dad's conflicted feelings about Phil were similar to his conflicted attitude toward his brother Harry. I don't agree, but Russ and I heard from my dad many times, "If your word is no good, you are no good." That's part of why Phil's counselor's advice was so valuable. His reminder that to an alcoholic lying is like breathing, a way to survive, gave me a more nuanced perspective than my dad's black-and-white statement.

Whether or not Phil ever got control of or understood his dependency remains an open question in our family. I want to say yes, but even late in life, he still believed he was the one alcoholic who could have a drink or two and stop. Though, obviously, when you end up in detox multiple times, it should be a wakeup call. Phil had times in his life when he spent a couple nights with homeless people because there was no alternative. So he had some experiences that should have been a warning he had hit the bottom rung of the ladder. It was obvious when Phil was drinking. Toward the end of his life, I talked to him once a week. I saw no evidence he was drinking then.

I'm still amazed at how he would recover from situations where I would think he would be dead. He was in a hospital in Florida for over six months battling problems with his kidney. Then he got a staph infection that often kills people. When I went to visit him, he was unconscious the entire time. I was afraid someone was going to ask if I wanted to pull the plug. But the surgeon assured that he was in an induced coma, which made me wonder if they'd induced the coma because Phil would be a terrible patient. "Ultimately I think he'll walk out of here," the surgeon told me. And he did.

Phil visited us in Minnesota every summer. I always arranged the flights because he didn't have the patience to talk to people. He wouldn't have done it online either—but before that was an option, you had to call and wait on the phone, holding and holding, to buy plane tickets. So I'd set up his flights, and then I'd end up paying for them too, because he never had money. He would stay at our home in Lakeville for a couple of days and then we'd drive him up to Duluth to see our mother and he would stay there for a bit. Then we'd go back to get him and take him back to the airport. His favorite part of the trip was checking out the Schneiderman's stores. He would hang with me for days and listen in on conversations. He was all over it.

I appreciate my wife, Sheila, not just for putting up with Phil, but also for insisting he stay with us. As a houseguest, you couldn't host anyone worse than him. My wife would make nice dinners and he would never say thank you. To give you an idea of the type of guest he was, one night we had a bunch of the family over for a nice steak dinner. I grilled the steaks. There were 11 of us and my wife was commenting over dinner that she had gotten 10 steaks—they only had 10 left—at Von Hanson's, our butcher, so she picked up the other one at Cub Foods.

"I must have gotten the one from Cub," Phil replied.

Then he disappeared later in the evening before the other guests left. That's what he would do—dominate and then disappear. I went to check on him. "Are you okay?" I asked.

"Yeah, I'm just reading." He was an unbelievably avid reader.

"Everybody thinks you must have been bored."

"Well, you could say that."

He also wouldn't clean up after himself. My wife described him as a combination of needy and demanding. It was irritating.

On one of Phil's last visits, he brought a camera and was taking pictures of our house and our gardening to share with our cousin in Florida. It was an awkward moment for me, so I offered, "Phil, sometimes I'm almost embarrassed by everything I have: the family, the business, the house . . . so much."

He looked at me and asked, "Larry, do you know the difference between envy and jealousy?"

I didn't.

"Envy says, I wish I had that. Jealousy says, I wish I had yours. I'm envious, but I'm not jealous. You made good choices. I made bad choices."

Over the years, I've observed employees who, like Phil, were exceptionally intelligent. Several of those folks, also like Phil, self-destructed as employees. I've heard others say they lack common sense. Art Mortell, author and consultant, attributes this tendency to a lack of "sensibility." When a person is missing that set of coping skills, they tend to be unaware of or unable to understand their emotions—and thus how their emotional life influences their everyday reality. One of the tests we use for job applicants is a general intelligence test. Over the years, we have not enjoyed a great track record with employees of exceptional intelligence. I would love to know whether serious studies of employee intelligence in various industries confirm our experience.

One of the things Phil did often was call Mom, which was appreciated.

Unfortunately, his calls sometimes became requests for financial assistance. His teeth needed a lot of work and he had a number of health concerns. After several months without working, he'd decide to get back into the workforce. However, in order to do that, he needed, at various times, to see the dentist, buy medication, buy clothes, and other things to get started. Phil knew Mom and I liked the idea of him going back to work, so frequently that was the rationale for his financial needs.

At one point, Mom had an insurance policy that was maturing and Phil was going to inherit some money. We knew this would be poison for Phil, so Mom and I devised a strategy through which we could help Phil with his requests and still be fair to Claudia and Karen. So, when Phil asked Mom for money, she would call me and let me know how much he needed. I had set up a checking account especially for these requests and when the policy matured, the amount Phil had received from the account was eventually deducted from his proceeds.

My mother looked at things differently than my dad did. She was very aware of Phil's problems *and* his feelings, but she also had a more forgiving and nonjudgmental nature than my dad. Dad could really hold a grudge. My mom just wasn't that way. She would be more hopeful. She wasn't blind to Phil's issues and problems—but she loved him, and there's no doubt he loved her deeply too.

My mother often said, "I wish there was something we could have done differently with Phil." I don't think there's anything more they could have done. They did their best with him, just as they did with David.

For all of Phil's demons and issues, I loved him dearly and I miss him. I could call him day or night and he would give me plenty to think about. Sometimes too much.

7

Expansion into the Twin Cities

I wanted the challenge of a multi-store business. We were already doing well at our Meadowlands store. The first economic slump we faced was in 1982, when the iron ore industry took a huge nosedive on the Iron Range due to a lack of demand. There were many layoffs in the mining industry and among other businesses that depended on it. At that point, we were debt free. Every year during the 1970s, our business had grown in sales, but in one year alone, 1982, we dropped over $300,000 from 1981. We had to solve the question of how we were going to maintain our business. We determined that we had to get a bigger part of the Duluth market to be successful, so we opened a fairly small store in Duluth. By opening that store, we could service our customers without expanding our warehouse or buying more trucks. We could test the waters into expansion. The experience took some of the mystery out of the idea of expanding. That was an easy deal and was successful enough. Our volume increased, and so did our expenses, but we were profitable.

At the time we expanded into the Duluth market, Schneiderman's Furniture had never held a promotional sale. So we decided to play on that for an advertisement. I still have a great picture of that ad—it's my favorite Schneiderman's ad of all time. It shows my mother, Russell, and me on one side of a couch with big smiles on our faces. My dad was on the other end of the couch with a curmudgeonly expression, which came naturally to him. The headline said, "Three out of four Schneidermans think a sale is a good idea." He was upset, very upset, about the clearance sale and yet, when asked, he took his place on the sofa for the newspaper ad. A longer than usual silent treatment followed that incident. He thought we had completely abrogated the core values he lived by. We received tremendous feedback from our customers about that ad, though. They liked that our family was in the ad. The message resonated and was successful. We had taken the first step down that slippery slope and we continued to have sales. Often, in fact.

Shortly after we opened the Duluth store 1982, we heard a long-time and well-known retailer in Lakeville, Gephart's Furniture, had gone out of business, leaving their building vacant. Lakeville is a Twin Cities suburb about 20 miles south of Minneapolis, and Gephart's was a highly respected business there dating back to the late 1890s. After we heard from a number of people about how great the location was, we drove down to the Twin Cities with our banker, Jerry Jubie. Jerry said he would back us. He was enthusiastic, thought it was a good deal, and encouraged us to buy the building, which we did.

In hindsight, we were fortunate to do as well as we did. We didn't do market studies or any kind of research into where we were locating our store, or if we had enough target clientele. We weren't known at all in the market. While we had started advertising in a limited way two years earlier when we opened the Duluth store, we lacked marketing know-how. We felt vaguely confident in our ability to compete, though. At the time, Gabbert's and Dayton's represented the higher quality, price, and service story. The lower quality, price, and service merchants were Slumberland, Levitz, and Wickes. We were in the middle, along with several other strong independents.

One of our best early moves was recruiting Rich Allen as our manager/merchandiser at Lakeville. He had been a successful furniture manager at Dayton's and had a keen sense of the market. He brought experience and skill in merchandising and advertising. It was a tough day for me when Rich resigned to move to San Francisco to become a financial manager. However, before he left, he did some research and recommended another Dayton's manager, Rich Carl. Rich became our general manager and brought with him excellent skills and ideas in regards to employee-customer relationships. Rich, as much as anyone I ever worked with, embraced learning, created a positive work environment, and helped us grow in many ways. One of the best things Rich did for Schneiderman's was finding Susan Strong, our current merchandise manager.

We knew that with our higher overhead in the Lakeville location, we couldn't afford to wait for word of mouth to make us successful, but we didn't have any particular niche in the market, we were unknown, and we didn't have a consistent advertising message. Then, like now, good advertising was vital. It was Phil who told me it might be a good idea to find out who was behind the ads for Titus McDuff, a men's clothing retailer. Their message resonated with us. I did a little research that led us to a collaboration with a Minneapolis agency owned by Dean and Dan Oberpriller, twin brothers who were long on passion and drive, and had a big dose of attitude. The brothers were relentless in advocating their ideas, which provided some interesting dynamics with the three Schneiderman brothers.

At the time, furniture stores utilized newspaper ads almost

exclusively. We had a photographer take several shots of my dad and then the Oberprillers wrote no-nonsense, cleverly worded ads featuring my father saying things like: "I don't care if you don't buy your furniture from us. It's your home." So there was Dad, who never believed in advertising, getting a big kick out of the ads. They were spot on.

The Oberprillers helped us create an identity. One billboard concept that got a lot of comments—positive and negative—proclaimed, "We love Dayton's and Gabbert's, that's where a lot of our customers come from!" It was signed, "Max Schneiderman."

One afternoon in 1984, just after we opened the Lakeville store, Russ and I were doing some competitive shopping at Dayton's in Edina. We had coats and ties on, and so we looked like salespeople. One of the shoppers asked, "Can I get this dresser in a different size?"

We looked around for a salesperson—honest, we did—but none could be found. So my brother responded, "Yes, as a matter of fact you can get it in a different size. You can get it in 60-inch and 52-inch sizes."

"How much is it?" she asked.

We came clean then, and told the two women we had our own furniture store in Lakeville.

"Well, maybe I should come out there and look," she replied.

"If you want to," I said, "that would be great, but I feel a bit strange about the whole situation."

She smiled and whispered, "I won't tell anybody."

Russ and I made one quick stop on our way back to downtown Lakeville. When we arrived back at the store, here were the two women from Dayton's. One of them looked at me, put a finger in front of her mouth, and said, "Shhh." I took it as a good indication that we'd made the right decision to expand into the Twin Cities.

The woman, who lived in Minnetonka, was our first large order in Lakeville: $10,000. I think in those days you probably could have made a lot of money hanging around Dayton's.

Our next new location was in Minnetonka in 1987—a 25,000-square-foot building adjoining a K-Mart. The Roseville store was our third building in the Twin Cities; it has 41,000 square feet and opened in 1990. Then in 1991, we moved our Lakeville store closer to I-35W and expanded to 80,000 square feet. In 1994, we built a 35,000-square-foot store in Woodbury. The smaller size of that store was a factor of the available lot size. In 1999, we built a location in Maple Grove, also 35,000 square feet, because the size had worked well in Woodbury. The store was beautiful and is still doing well.

In hindsight, we would have been more efficient if all of our showrooms were the same size and layout with the same square footage and design—like other chain stores do. Uniformity of size and layout in multiple locations means display and merchandising can be duplicated. This is not only cost effective, but causes less confusion for customers when they visit more than one location. Many of our decisions about the design of our stores were determined by what was available based on location and cost, and by what the competition dictated.

Compared to our competitors HOM Furniture and Becker Furniture, we had much smaller stores. It didn't take long for us to see the side effect of our competitions' larger stores. Soon after we built the new store in Maple Grove, our major competitor HOM Furniture built their flagship store in Plymouth, right between our Maple Grove and Minnetonka locations. We couldn't compete with their selection, so we built a 110,000-square-foot store in Plymouth in 2006, and closed our two smaller stores in Maple Grove and Minnetonka. Meanwhile, HOM built a large showroom in Duluth, so that same year we countered with a new 55,000-square-foot showroom near the

Miller Hill Mall.

To a large extent, the growth followed our overall plan. Initially, when Russ and I opened the Lakeville store in 1984, we thought additional stores in the north, east, and west suburbs would make sense. After Russ and Monica lost their son Joey to leukemia on February 24, 1985, they decided to remain in the Twin Cities, allowing Russ to manage our Minnetonka and Roseville locations at various times. Russ loved building things and he worked tirelessly during construction projects. Having him on the scene during construction and set-up benefitted us greatly.

The second recession that affected us was in 2005 and 2006, when we were in the middle of building projects in Plymouth and Duluth. Part of our challenge was that HOM had built stores near every one of our locations in the Twin Cities. They are an aggressive company, but we had locations in great areas: Lakeville, Roseville, and—at the time—Maple Grove and Woodbury. They were all fast-growing, affluent suburbs.

One of the lessons we learned during our growth phases in the Twin Cities is that our loyal customer base would still buy from us. But new customers (and even some people who had bought from us in the past) were tempted away by the *great, big brand-new store nearby.* It is exciting to go and look at new things. Eventually, our business in Duluth and Meadowlands dropped severely when HOM opened its new store in Duluth. In addition, our sales in Maple Grove dropped. My brother Russ and I looked at our various options and we decided if we wanted to remain in business and grow (but, more pointedly, remain in business), we needed to build a competitive store in Plymouth *and* in Duluth. These were big, expensive locations that required multimillion-dollar loans. Both locations cost us a lot more than was projected. In Plymouth, due to the previous owner's use of chemicals, we had to deal with expensive pollution issues, which meant we needed to work with the Minnesota Pollution Control Agency, and the Environmental Protection Agency. The bank needs assurance if something happens to Schneiderman's and the building has to be sold; they don't want to deal with a devalued property that isn't clean. This process resulted in long delays and significant additional expense.

In order to meet building code requirements for the City of Duluth, we had to make major construction changes. We built the store at an excellent location right next to the mall. But it is on rocks. Neither the city water nor the city sewer reached the location. We knew about the water and sewer lines in advance, and we had engineers investigate. We weren't *that* foolish, but it turned out to be much more expensive to blast through those rocks and install the water and sewer systems than the engineers estimated—partly as a result of delays caused by the city's inspection process. After every day of blasting through the stone, Duluth required a city inspector to review the work before we were allowed to move on. The frequent inspections meant delays, but also additional costs since we were responsible for the expense of the inspections.

I have to admit there were times when I wondered if we'd open those stores because they were enormously expensive. Adding to the frustration, we were working with a larger national bank with extreme employee turnover. We had three different account managers during the building period, which caused delays and added to the overall cost. I finally got to the point with the bank that I went above our business manager and told *his* manager the incompetence we experienced had cost us upwards of $100,000 and I needed him to be directly involved or I was going to go farther up the chain. It didn't take long for things to get better.

We were dealing with unprecedented issues with the economy combined with normal business challenges in a lean company, while building two huge buildings in Duluth and Plymouth. In my career so far, 2006 and 2007 were the most difficult years. I went as far as speculating about what new job I might take up if we sold or closed the business. While enjoying lunch with a good friend of mine who was employed by the Red Cross, I shared my thoughts about what I would do if I wasn't in the furniture business. He commented that I would be great as an executive in a nonprofit organization. I smiled and quipped, "I've been doing that for over 30 years."

In January 2007, we moved our business from the large national bank chain to Bremer Bank, still a big business, but more oriented to smaller, family businesses. We could immediately see a difference in stability and a stronger focus on relationships. This was a tough recessionary period and a challenging time for furniture retailers. Many people think the furniture business goes up and down with housing. There's some truth to that, but the true barometer is the Consumer Confidence Index. If consumers aren't confident of their financial situation, they don't usually buy good furniture. The higher-quality furniture manufacturers and retailers are hit harder in recessionary times than those making and selling lower-quality furniture. As an industry spokesperson put it, "In the good, better, and best of furniture retailers, the good have done the best." They aren't as susceptible to economic difficulties as higher-end retailers. At the time, gas prices were also hurting peoples' spending habits, and it affected their pocketbooks and their confidence. It was the first time in my career when we needed to seriously cut our expenses, which meant laying off a number of people. Looking back, I waited too long before I began the difficult job of getting our expenses in line for lower business expectations. I had hoped the economy would improve and we wouldn't need to make the cuts. This was the first time I dealt with a bank when things weren't going so well.

Despite my personal worries, Schneiderman's was still solid. That was due to one of the key business principles my dad instilled in us—Russ and I were both conservative. Even as we were building those stores, we had a strong balance sheet. It was the income statement that caught the bank's attention. Banking is a business, of course, and we had a big mortgage. With a global economic crisis at hand and with retail a particularly troubled category, the bank became concerned about its investment. Several large furniture chains had gone bankrupt. Though our balance sheet remained strong, like most retailers, a significant percentage of our assets is always tied up in inventory. For good reasons, banks aren't comfortable with inventory as collateral. When banks are forced to take inventory as payment toward loans, they typically need to hire a company to liquidate and the goods are often sold for 25 percent of the wholesale value—or less.

Well, suddenly, we were involved in ratios that had never been of concern since we had always met or exceeded them. It's interesting banks refer to these ratios as covenants. If the borrower doesn't meet these numbers, then the covenant is not met. At this point, technically, the business becomes "in default."

Despite our expensive (on many levels) experience at the national bank, one person there worked hard to help us. Just before we left that bank, he left and joined Bremer. After several conversations, we moved all of our business and Ryan Welle managed our account. I was impressed by his business sense and, in time, we became friends.

Ryan told me, "We need *you* to go to an asset-based lender."

So, I asked him what an "asset-based lender" is. He said it is basically what it sounds like. They specialize in loans based on collateral such as inventory. Their interest rates are going to be higher, but many businesspeople swear by them. We discussed the probable implications further.

"Why don't you give me a name to start with?" I said. "Somebody you recommend, and I'll go from there."

Before he left, Ryan turned and said, "Larry, I want you to know all of us at the bank have total confidence in you and your company. These are scary times."

I met with Joel, the asset-based lender Ryan had recommended, and he was great. But it became obvious to me he was used to working with troubled businesses. For one thing, I would lose a degree of control. Their approval would be required prior to writing a single check above a specified amount. That had no appeal to me. The interest rates would be much higher, inventory audits would be performed quarterly at all of our locations, including the distribution center, *and we would have to pay for them.*

When all was said and done, this was a good guy to work with, but . . .

"Joel, it appears to me our expenses will go up about $160,000 a year."

He said, "I'm not surprised."

I was sick about it. Keep in mind, we have never been late with a payment—ever! I contacted a banker I know from another bank and asked for some other suggestions. He gave me a couple of names.

One was another asset-based lender, but there were no discernible savings. They wanted our business, which is always a good sign. But I couldn't help wondering why Bremer was forcing us to do this. Here we were at some kind of tipping point, struggling like crazy to make sense of everything, but we had a plan. It didn't make any sense to me. I bypassed my guy and bypassed his boss and his boss's boss, and I called the president of Bremer Bank, Steve Meads.

I had met Steve twice. Once when they first solicited our business, and then again when they got our business. "Love to have you with us," he'd said. "We love to have businesses like

Schneiderman's."

I didn't have a personal relationship with him outside those two meetings, but I called him up and said, "I don't know how familiar you are with our account"—they're a big bank, after all—"but I'm wondering if you have some time to talk to me."

"Well, of course, Larry," he replied. "You're a great customer. Next week I'll be here Thursday or Friday. Where would you like to meet?"

"All I want is 20 minutes of your time. I'd like to get together as soon as I can. There's a Dunn Brothers Coffee by your office. When can you meet me for 20 minutes?"

"Well, it's not right that you have to come all the way out here. You're my customer, I'll come out there. I can't do it until next week."

"You know what? You'd be doing me a favor. How about this afternoon? Do you have 20 minutes for me this afternoon?"

"Sure."

So we met at the coffee shop. We shook hands, said hello, and then I took my watch off, put it on the table, and said, "Steve, I'm going to honor this 20 minutes."

"Larry, don't worry about it."

"No, no. We'll be done in 20 minutes. Here's the deal. . . ." I explained my concerns about the asset-based lender. "I got to thinking about that. How will Schneiderman's going to an asset-based lender be in Bremer's best interest? The move would increase our expenses by $160,000 or more a year. That much money could be a tipping point for our business. Obviously you want us to succeed, because you hold the mortgages for these buildings. Further, we have plans to finish the lease at our Burnsville outlet and then having a big store-closing sale. We'll save all that overhead. We're going to close the Meadowlands store. When we close Meadowlands, we'll be able to close the second warehouse we have up there. We're going to deliver from our Burnsville distribution center. I'm not going to get into detail with how we'll restructure, but we have thought through our business plans and we're going to do it. Why this rush to push us to an asset-based lender?"

"I wish I knew more about your account," Steve said. "I didn't know this was happening. Could I look into it and call you next week?"

"Absolutely." I lifted my watch and said, "Now that's 20 minutes."

"How's everything else going?" he asked.

"You know what? I've never experienced the kind of stress I've had with this, and it spills over. I think about it all the time."

"Well, I can't make any guarantees right now, but let me try to de-stress you a little bit." As Steve prepared to go, he asked, "Larry, what would you say to somebody if you were asked, 'What do you think of Bremer Bank?'"

I thought for a couple seconds and then said, "I would say the people at Bremer are great and they stuck with me through thick."

Steve smiled, and said, "Not thin, though. I understand. We'll see if we can change that."

I felt good about the meeting. Late that afternoon, my wife and I were driving north to our cabin near Meadowlands. I have a bad habit of checking my voicemails once we get rolling north on 35W and my wife is asleep. There were two new messages.

One was from Ryan. "Larry, I want to tell you, I could never have suggested you do what you did, but I think it was an astute move on your part. I don't want to get into too much, but Steve Meads came back from the meeting and he got a bunch of people together and said I want to know everything about Schneider-man's on Monday. I think it was a really good idea on your part." Well, that was encouraging.

The other message was from one of Ryan's managers. "Larry, it took a lot of courage for you to go to Steve." I thought that was strange, because it really didn't take courage at all. "I hope you know I have always been in your court. I've always had a lot of respect for you and your operations, but these are tough times and retail furniture is a tough category. I hope you understand that, and I'm wishing you well with everything."

In the middle of the next week Ryan at Bremer called to say, "We'll keep your loan at Bremer. You're right; asking you to go to an asset-based lender is not a good move for the bank either."

It was a scare, but it all worked out. We moved forward with less stress than we had started with the previous week. Steve Meads was able to be a real banker. It was a win–win all around, except for the asset-based lender.

My dad, being an old Navy man, used to say to me, "Calm seas, never a great sailor made." I think that's true.

This period of time was a big transition for us, and we staved off serious potential problems by making critical decisions, starting with the closing of stores. Our Burnsville outlet store was a losing proposition. We learned a couple of things from running an outlet store. One is that it led to bad decisions. For instance, a vocal and demanding customer may be unhappy with their sofa that is a year and a half old. So, we would take it back and send it to the outlet. It was a bad decision. Then multiply that same scenario many times over. Successful outlets buy merchandise to sell. We did very little of that and we weren't good at it, either. It wasn't profitable, and it carried an expensive operating lease and eight employees. With the end of the lease in sight, we had a big, store-closing sale. People are attracted to store-closing events and this was no different. It went well and we were able to convert the store's inventory into cash. The salespeople at the outlet were given an opportunity to work at one of our other locations.

Our original location in Elmer township, which had expanded so many times, had been a financial drain for years. When we built the new Duluth store in 2006, there was no reason for Duluth/Superior–area customers to drive out to Meadowlands. The economy in the cities north of the store tends to shift up and down resulting in low consumer confidence. Most of these more cautious customers preferred to drive to Duluth where they could combine a furniture purchase with other tasks and shopping. I had engaged in wishful thinking for years, not wanting to close the store my parents had started. But at this point we could no longer afford to keep it open.

The Meadowlands store also had a big closing sale, which was fabulous since you can imagine the large number of customers and the amount of inventory from all of those years of doing business up there. We hated to do it. It was difficult, and we also had to close the warehouse up there. We had a position for a manager and display person in Duluth and one sales consultant. We also retained our delivery drivers because they would continue to deliver in northern Minnesota. Aside from one other offer of employment, we had nothing available for the rest of the Meadowlands staff. In particular, we were unable to offer positions to two longer-term employees. That was especially difficult.

In 1999, Russ and I joined a performance group. The automobile industry a long time ago realized the benefit of non-competing retailers getting together as peer groups. By sharing ideas and best practices, individual members grow and improve. Ted Shepherd, a furniture industry consultant, organized furniture retailers in a similar manner. The goal was to enable furniture retailers to come together and mutually benefit from their collective experience. Members have similar profiles in non-competing markets, and the group helps them build professional and personal relationships in a setting where best practices are shared. Originally, some of the groups had only four members, but now I believe all have 12 or more non-competing stores. We meet three times per year in various locations, generally the cities of the group members.

Each member is required to send in their company's financial information prior to the meetings and it is organized so the group can compare all the various financial measurements and see who is strong, and who needs help.

The meetings also have a best-idea session. Each member store contributes $50 in cash, and the two ideas with the most votes share the prize money. Schneiderman's has often implemented some of the "best ideas" we've heard from our performance group, and some of our colleagues have implemented *our* best ideas as well.

During a typical meeting, we visit and get fairly deep into discussions about members' stores and distribution centers. Then we share constructive criticism. If you happen to be hosting the group at your store, the constructive criticism often develops into a rapid river of advice. It starts off with some positives. Then the group tends to tentatively offer suggestions. Finally, nearly everybody is pointing out your flaws, which might range from housekeeping needs, to merchandising, to displays, to your employees, or anything else out of order that someone noticed. It can be overwhelming, and visits to our facilities used to drive Russ up a tree. The best course of action is to keep your head down, listen politely, keep expressing your thanks, and write down the ideas you agree with.

One of the group's most important exercises was that nobody would leave the three-day meeting without sharing what goals they hoped to accomplish by the next meeting. Russ and I made numerous changes to the business as a result of the commitments we made at these meetings. The same has been true more recently with Jason and me.

Shepherd later sold the company to Bob George, and Bob has improved the organization. While Ted was challenging, and even abrasive, if I ever see him again, I would certainly shake his hand

and thank him. What we've learned and implemented through the groups has made a huge difference for our company—and you can't overstate the value of good networking. Frequently, when issues have come up, it's been easy and helpful to pick up the phone and bounce ideas around with other members of our group. During the extremely difficult business conditions in 2007–08, we were able to put much of what we learned from our colleagues to practical use.

A significant example of implementing an idea we gleaned from our group participation is when we replaced the warehouse in Meadowlands by purchasing what's called the demountable truck system, which allows us to perform our deliveries in northern Minnesota through our Burnsville distribution center. We learned about the system through Joe Fonti in our performance group, and saw the system in use for Wisconsin Furniture and Appliance Mart at their outlying locations. Two delivery boxes are designed so that you can walk right through the first one to load the second one on a semitrailer frame. These boxes are brought to Duluth overnight by our semi, dropped off, and then hitched to two smaller delivery trucks. Then the semi returns to Burnsville with two empty delivery boxes—and this process is repeated four times per week. The demountable truck system is, essentially, a warehouse on wheels.

Closing the Burnsville outlet store, the Meadowlands store, and the warehouse meant we were able to eliminate two stores that were losing money, and then sell or redistribute the remaining warehouse inventory. We paid off our line of credit and, for the most part, we haven't needed it since. To use my dad's metaphor, navigating those less-than-calm seas was difficult, but hopefully it made us better sailors.

The closings meant laying off employees. We used the same format with each employee we needed to lay off throughout the company. I, along with the employee's manager, met with the person and let him or her know that the decision didn't reflect on their performance, that it was an economic necessity. We offered a modest severance package. Prior to each meeting, I would remind myself we had no choice and silently say a prayer for that person.

Some reactions surprised me, but I reminded myself that next to a death in your family, more stress is caused by losing your job than most anything else. Most of our employees saw the layoffs coming with the slowdown of sales, so while people may not have been surprised, some were still in shock.

Up until this time, I never had to lay off anybody for lack of work. Many years before, when we had the recession on the Iron Range, I needed to cut the hours of our warehouse staff in Meadowlands from 40 to 32. I remember being nervous and feeling bad when I met with the employees, but I was surprised at how well they reacted to the news. However, once the staff received their checks, a couple of them were angry because they didn't realize their checks were going to be cut along with their hours. I guess I didn't communicate that clearly, but I thought it would be obvious. Lesson learned; take nothing for granted.

The store closings and layoffs were steps we had to take; the company needed to make those moves to weather the recession.

I'll never forget a phone call with my mom as I was on my way to the store-closing sale in Meadowlands, which started on a Thursday. I figured the closing of the store there would be a big disappointment for her. As we talked, I mentioned how terrible I felt about it and that I expected to see a lot of long-time customers. "You know what?" she said. "It's not like one of your kids has cancer or something." That sure put things in perspective.

8

Vendors and Sales Reps

My parents taught me to appreciate and respect the vendors and sales reps who called on us. Initially, Mom and Dad bought very little furniture, and their store was way off the beaten path. The former would change; the latter did not. In those early days, my parents truly appreciated these reps calling on them. Sales reps were especially important because we were so far from anything, and they would take the time to come out and bring us up to date with the outside world. My father did the buying, but Mom often made suggestions. At a fairly young age, I could tell that my dad often made sympathy buys from the few reps who made the pilgrimage to Elmer. It's a good thing Dad was a good salesman, because sometimes he would buy some items that were a stretch—and he had a penchant for buying too much.

For the most part, we have enjoyed great relationships with our vendors. Unfortunately, dealing with what was once our most important brand—Thomasville Furniture—taught us some painful lessons. Perhaps the greatest lesson that came out of the experience was a clear vision of who we wanted to be as a company.

Thomasville was one of the top names in the furniture industry, but Russ and I began tiring of their demands. Who was the customer here anyway? They were our largest vendor and, at retail, we were doing more than $8 million in sales with them annually. Somewhere along the way, Thomasville executives decided they wanted to be another Ethan Allen. They de-emphasized in-store galleries and focused their efforts on opening exclusive, free-standing Thomasville stores, the same approach Ethan Allen had taken with their brand. While Ethan Allen is indeed successful, I can't name another furniture brand that has been able to market themselves well enough to have real success with their own stores. Brands trend hot and cold among consumers, and most vendors understand that it isn't easy making a profit in retail furniture.

We had between 5,000 and 8,500 square feet of Thomasville furniture in every Schneiderman's showroom, plus we had a Thomasville-exclusive store in Bloomington. Thomasville withdrew their advertising and discount support, which had always been important to us. Suddenly it seemed that in order for us to enjoy any of the benefits of being a good customer, we needed to open Thomasville-branded stores. We no longer felt appreciated for the business we were giving them.

Our Thomasville representative resigned and they hired a new sales rep. Meanwhile, they continued to push us to open additional Thomasville-only stores. Since we only had one relatively small Thomasville store, it did make sense if they were going to be successful in this approach, to open at least three more in the Twin Cities. Two of their executives came up and met with me and our new sales rep. It was a one-sided conversation. As they got ready to leave, they asked the rep to join them for a private discussion. I could see the executives talking animatedly with him outside, while he said very little. When they left, the rep came back inside and his face was flushed. I asked him what was going on and he told me the sales manager had told him if he didn't meet his quota in this territory he was going to find the toe of his boot up his ass. Nice people.

While things continued to heat up, Russ and I made a big mistake. Our rep told us Thomasville wanted us to fly to St. Louis to see their new store layout. Once we got there, we began sharing ideas back and forth with the storeowner and his Thomasville rep. We all agreed we would exchange ideas with each other and the conversation would be confidential. I remember Russ and I felt the time was well spent and we had shared a number of thoughts. The next day, our rep called me and told me management was "thoroughly pissed" because of the negativity expressed at that meeting. He repeated a couple of things that made it plain our conversation was anything but confidential. The St. Louis Thomasville rep wasn't returning my calls. Eventually, I got a hold of her and she said she was sorry, but she needed this job and management had wanted to know everything we had said, or else.

We didn't believe in that business philosophy. And, anyway, did we want to become Thomasville rather than Schneiderman's?

I told Russ I could see no way they were going to change their direction and we agreed that we would be smarter to get out of the Thomasville line on our terms instead of waiting for their demands. Life is too short. Business should be fun.

It became plain to Thomasville that we were not going to open more stores featuring only their brand, so they made an offer to a competitor to do so. Thomasville came back to us prior to making a deal with the other company and gave us one last chance, but we declined and wished them well. At this point, we began a major merchandising change. We needed to close out large amounts of Thomasville furniture and find replacements for our largest vendor. We liked the new level of independence and not having to depend on them. Ultimately, our competitor didn't do well and they no longer carry the line. It was a big loss of sales for Thomasville.

A decade later, Schneiderman's is a Thomasville retailer once again. It's a new company with new challenges and new leaders. Our initial results are promising. Still, Russ would be shaking his head at this turn of events.

Over the years sales reps have had a tough time. One of the noteworthy challenges is that strong and charismatic reps have the potential to make more money than their managers do. It can become a matter of contention, partly because good sales reps often do not have strong attention to detail. Therefore the people who need to manage the sales and fix problems caused by that lack of detail can harbor some animosity toward the offending reps. Reps aren't often appreciated much by retailers, because with only rare exceptions, they'll sell us anything we want to buy. This becomes a problem when we buy a line of furniture, only to find the rep has just sold the same line to our competitor. Now, we could compete on price, but do we want to be selling the exact same furniture? Not really, and our sales reps know this. It can be irritating at times. In fact, this happened once with HOM Furniture. When they found out we had ordered the same pieces, they asked if we would carry something else. When things like that happen, it can put the sales rep in an awkward position.

Despite problems like this, I can't help but find a great appreciation for them. Several of my good friends today are reps—guys I've known a long time. They have been a big part of the fun of working in this industry.

There are three points I would like to make about sales reps: they are underappreciated, they are important, and they have contributed to my love of the business.

Since we began selling furniture, we have had more sales reps than I could possibly count. Many of them taught me a lot about attitude, professionalism, and the business itself. Pat Quirk, who represented Hammary, comes to mind as one of the first reps my parents genuinely considered a friend. He was a classy guy who had a flair for merchandising. Some of his calls to the store were around lunchtime and Pat would come upstairs and my mom or Claudia would make him lunch. Pat would point out which products large retailers were selling and he helped teach my dad the basics of merchandising. He even made suggestions on how we could improve our display. He added a helpful new technique with me. He would make display suggestions and then when he showed up the next time, we would wander out on the floor and he would generally compliment me on display updates. Then I'd buy his living room tables—lots of them. Remembering Pat, I can't help but appreciate how much he mentored me. His experience in setting up displays propelled me forward in that regard, helping me understand the importance of presentation.

It's not surprising Pat's two sons became sales reps themselves, and later became owners of a successful upholstery company. This was exactly the way of sales reps for decades. It was more than a job for them; often it became a family legacy.

In writing this book, I recall more and more people I want to mention, people who have been an important part of my career over the past 50 years. Many of them are sales reps. Here are a few of my favorites.

Joe Lipkin

Joe represented Ello, and was already up there in age when he called on my parents in the early 1960s. This man was a real gentleman and he had a spell on my mom, who purchased the wall accessories. Mom would buy large amounts of wall art and to sell it, she used a technique successful sales consultants still use. Once a customer bought a sofa, Mom would ask, "What are you going to put on the wall over it?" Almost every customer needed something and Mom would bring out two pieces of art that were especially fitting, and often, they would buy one. Joe continued to work as a sales rep until he was close to 90. One day he was in the store, with his notebook open. I asked him what he was writing and he said that for every store, he recorded the buyers' names and the best times to make calls. I noticed a little map on the page and asked him what it was. He looked up and said, "Why, that's where the bathroom is."

Al Luke

Al represented several lines—Burlington House, United, and Globe—and was a real salesman. Once my parents and I began attending the Dallas Market, Al would insist on taking us out for dinner. In fact, he would invite several dealers to those dinners, and some of them became our friends. Al was the first rep who insisted on presenting sales meetings at our store. We tended to consider his products first and we sold a lot of them, which was no coincidence. Al's son, Mike, has been successful as a furniture rep as well, which tends to be a theme in this line of work—the family tradition, so to speak.

Don Mahlow

For sheer goofiness, I miss guys like Don Mahlow. Don represented La-Z-Boy and Null. He was an older guy when we first met him. Don had a caustic edge, but he was funny. One day he called and told me he wanted to show me the new La-Z-Boy recliner styles the next day. I said that was fine, but I had to leave the store no later than 3:00. He said there would be plenty of time. The next day, it's 2:40 and no Don. I told Bob, my brother-in-law, that when and if Don showed up, to let him know he missed me and remind him I had told him I would be gone by 3:00. As we're having this discussion, in walks Don. He says hello, puts his catalogs and fabrics on the table, announces he needs to use the "can," and takes off. I figured I would wait for him to return and remind him that I needed to leave, but before I can get a word in, he is pouring himself a coffee and complaining about how strong it looks. Finally I said, "Don, I told you I have to leave at 3:00. It's now a quarter to 3:00."

He sets his cup down with a disgusted look. "I'll be a goddamned son of a bitch! I bust my ass to get here from Minneapolis just to show a snot-nosed buyer how to make some money and this is what I get? Fifteen minutes? I'll tell you what, you can shove it up your a—"

"Don, now you have 12 minutes."

He said, "Okay, okay, here's what you need to see," and he showed us.

One day after Russ told him his other line looked like it was built for midgets, Don put his arm around my shoulder and said, "Larry, take care of yourself because if you die, he might be the buyer."

Sometimes, Don's wife would travel with him and that could create some interesting dynamics. He would recommend a fabric and she would say things like, "What woman would ever buy that ugly thing?" He would just look at her and smile. I wonder what he was thinking.

Dick O'Connor

Dick was our Drexel representative. He was Irish, funny, and had a colorful vocabulary. When we were teenagers and Russ and I saw his car parked at the store, we wanted to just listen to the guy. Mom tried to keep us busy and out of hearing range. We noticed Dad's language always got more colorful after Dick's visits. We weren't used to selling furniture in this upper price range, but we did okay with it. Despite representing a fairly high-end line, Dick never took himself too seriously. He could laugh at himself. Drexel had a nice accent collection called Et Cetera. One of the pieces was a little round cocktail table called The Lily. It was pretty, with a round glass top that sat on top of a gold base resembling a lily. Well, my dad pointed out they must not have been thinking when it was designed because the coarse finish looked terrible as you looked down through the glass top. And this was a pricey little table. When Dad pointed this out, Dick had a string of expletives about the lack of quality, and ordered a new base. The new base had the same problem, and so did the next attempt. On his next visit Dick tells us he made a strong statement at the sales meeting in North Carolina in front of all the management and other reps about quality issues. He cited The Lily table as evidence of the "don't give a shit," attitude he'd been seeing. At this point he was informed that he and his customer (my dad) were showing the base upside down. Whoops!

Milt Johnson

Milt was a diminutive man who represented Paoli Company. They had introduced a collection of nostalgic oak pieces. I liked Milt, and I liked the look of the pieces. What I didn't like was the price, which seemed too high. Yet, I admit to having some of my dad in me. So, I pointed at three items and decided to take a little chance with them. Milt said, "That's a problem. You need to buy 12 pieces to qualify. So, I exclaim, "Twelve pieces! What if they don't sell?"

"Well, no problem," Milt says. "You won't need to reorder then!"

There were guys (sales reps were always guys in the early days) who may not have had the sophistication of the characters on the *Mad Men* TV series, but some had their drinking habits. Not infrequently, these road warriors would come in slurring and smelling of booze. They knew my dad as a smart and funny down-to-earth guy, but they didn't know how much my dad despised talking to people who had been drinking. He had no patience for it, and would suddenly become too busy to talk with them. Dad would make a point to verbalize his disgust to Russ and me. We'd just be grateful he hadn't bought more inventory.

The furniture reps varied from a few who possessed questionable competence, to many more who showed a strong work ethic and professionalism.

We had a rep call on us at about 3:00 one afternoon. He drove a late-model white car and was wearing a pink shirt. I was the buyer for Schneiderman's at the time and I let him show me his line of sofas and chairs. We carried Flexsteel in similar styles and price points, so I told him that we didn't need this product, we were covered. He started to cry. He literally cried. That was a first, and I've never experienced a rep in tears since. The next day there was quite a hubbub in the village of Meadowlands. Some dude showed up at the school during cheerleading practice and exposed himself. It was reported he was wearing a pink shirt and may have been driving a late-model white car—more than odd.

With all of the different personalities over the years, it's important for me to mention an almost slam-dunk system some of the sales reps shared in the 1970s and 1980s. In that golden age of sales, many reps realized no matter what they did or how they acted, they had a product the stores needed. So they could make their own rules. One incident comes to mind that I find rather funny now, involving a sales rep who sold Keller. Our customers had been asking about a Keller dining line. Though Keller is no longer in business, they were a hot product for many years. Because the sales rep had never called on us, I was beginning to wonder if they had promised to sell their product exclusively through one of our competitors in Duluth. I wanted that line and knew they showed at the Minneapolis Furniture Market. So I committed to several sets and hoped the rep wouldn't tell me no. After he wrote up the sale, I asked him to do a sales meeting at our store in Meadowlands. "Aren't you north of Duluth?" he asked. I told him we were, and he announced, "I don't travel north of Minneapolis. I'm telling you that right now." He knew he didn't have to come to us to make a sale, and he never did.

Even though a few reps had a somewhat cavalier approach to sales, there were many sales reps who called on us with a professional demeanor. One who comes to mind is Monte McKie. He had been a buyer for Dayton's and he had strong fashion sense, but he also had strong selling skills and worked hard to sell us the right styles. I can't recall another rep who took the time to bring display layouts of our showroom to the furniture market to help us make new selections. He would also have recommendations waiting for us based on rate of sale and look of the new product.

Monte was always dressed to the nines. His tie had a perfect Windsor knot and if that wasn't enough, he wore a gold pin behind the knot with matching cuff links. After Monte had called on us for a long time and we'd developed a mutual like and respect, he resigned from his long-time employer, Thomasville Furniture. He was going to take a new position selling something we were unlikely to use. He was a bit emotional the day of his last sales call to our store, and he asked me if he could say goodbye to everyone. So, this fashion plate went to everyone's workstation and thanked each person. He had tears in his eyes afterward when he said to me, "That was hard." I asked him if he had just gone to the restroom and he hadn't. I complimented his sharp navy blue suit, but informed him that the fly on his slacks was wide open. He reached down, pulled the fly up, and said with a smile, "And you always say I'm a perfectionist." I knew we would miss him and we did.

Furniture manufacturers, like all businesses today, are driven to cut costs. They have to; competition is tough. Today, there are far, far fewer small furniture retailers, and much of the furniture sold is imported. That means lower prices on which reps earn lower commissions—and, typically, large orders are shipped by container at lower commission rates. So sales reps' incomes have decreased, while their traveling costs have increased. This has not created a formula for drawing bright young people into the business. Nor has it provided better service for retailers, especially smaller ones. Simply put, in many cases, reps can't afford to spend time and money servicing the smaller retailers. Some reps I've known have left the industry, but most love the furniture business as I do.

I have business friends, and I have personal friends in the furniture business. Some of these sales reps are throwbacks to a different era and they know it. One of those was Harry Bassett, who I considered one of my best long-time friends. After Harry passed away on February 22, 2013, I delivered his eulogy. He had provided plenty of material.

I first met Harry about 35 years ago when he was a mattress rep for King Koil. According to some, if there had been an 11th Commandment, it should have been, "And thou shalt not take thyself too seriously." Nobody I've met was a better evangelist of this notion than Harry. Right from the start, I was drawn to his sense of humor. As the years passed, I came to appreciate the depth of his feelings for many things in life, especially his wife, Gayle, his sons, Chris and Bryan, and later his grandchildren, his friends, his church, his Indian heritage, his cabin, and on and on. His sharp and sometimes biting wit meant sometimes he could be misinterpreted or underestimated, not that he cared.

We opened the Duluth store with Harry's mattress brand and Sealy. The Sealy rep had already had a meeting with the staff, and at that time, there was no question that Sealy was a superior product. When one of our sales consultants commented the Sealy mattresses were much heavier, indicating there was more in them, Harry responded, "We're the line who keeps the delivery man in mind." Next question, he was done.

We need the reps we buy from to help us with sales training. Harry was leading a meeting with a focus on a new sectional we had recently bought from the company he was representing. The company sold what we'd call promotional-quality products. One of the sales consultants kept asking Harry about construction details and comparing them to another brand we carry. "So, why would I sell this to a customer when it's almost as much as a Flexsteel?" he questioned Harry.

In exasperation, Harry answered, "Because Larry can make some money on this, okay?" After the meeting Harry seemed to have a trace of regret for responding in that way, but I'm not sure he really did. Another time, in a period when retail traffic was slow, I sent an email out with an attachment to all of our key reps, asking them not to dwell on negative things like slow traffic with our sales consultants because there was enough negativity out there without the reps adding to it. Moments later, I received a call from Harry. "Larry, great letter, but honestly, did you send a letter to all those people or just to me?"

Over the years, like the industry itself, Harry's sales and therefore his income had their ups and downs. He was let go from a company he had been with for a long time. It was particularly nasty, because he had partnered with his two boys. One of his sons continued on with the factory, but it created a tough situation. Regardless of the challenges over the years, Harry never talked about leaving the business.

Devastatingly, Harry got pancreatic cancer. I talked with him almost daily during his treatment and let him take the lead as far as the direction of the conversation. He commented, "I feel like I'm lucky when I see those young kids going through chemo."

"Well, you know, the Apostle Paul said to be thankful in all circumstances," I replied.

Harry, always keeping things light, retorted, "Well, I bet the Apostle Paul didn't have pancreatic cancer or a frigging furniture store!" God, I miss spending time with him.

One of the most important issues reps deal with is distribution. Most vendors, given a chance, would like to sell to every dealer, every outlet, that might boost their sales. That includes buying clubs, online retailers, wholesale clubs, and who knows what else. The problem with that is—why should a retailer invest in expensive floor space if a decent return can't be made? The way this works in general, is the bigger fish swallow the smaller fish. There are competitors we respect, but we don't want to share product. One example was a store called Furniture Minnesota. They were a long-time furniture retailer that eventually closed in 2009. Ironically, the owner, Steve Katainen, claims he patterned his store after Max Schneiderman's in Elmer, when he was a rep calling on my dad. I consider Steve a friend and I don't know if that's true or if he's just trying to annoy me. But his store was a true low-overhead situation with little inventory, no free delivery, no financing, and no advertising. As a larger dealer, we could avoid competing with his store if we wanted to by demanding the exclusive right to a particular furniture line. The same can happen to us when larger retailers sometimes shut us out from buying products we'd like to show. Some of the big retailers can tie up products and then never buy them after all, which is truly frustrating. The rep plays an important role in this process, attempting to do the best thing for the factory along with his own needs.

Imports have affected the industry in ways beyond the obvious. Distribution is a little less of an issue than in the past. There are few brand names in furniture today that enjoy consumer recognition. We conduct a significant business with Asian and Mexican container companies. We need to buy in quantity to make a profit, so a mistake can be expensive. Our major competitors import and often have copies made of popular styles at low prices. A downside of this situation is that there are fewer fresh and different styles, and more copies. An upside for the consumer is real value. In many cases, people buy furniture in 2013 for less than they paid 20 years ago, and sometimes it's better quality.

For example, when I was a teenager my father sold our accountant and his wife a house full of furniture. They wanted to buy something inexpensive for a spare bedroom and Dad sold them a brand called Styline, which was manufactured in Indiana. Dad wanted to make sure their expectations were in line with this promotional product. Our CPA got a good laugh when my dad told him we needed to tell our deliverymen not to show up at the door with the chest of drawers under one arm and the dresser under the other. There wasn't much to this stuff. Today, for about the same money, a consumer can get something more than decent. Of course, the product will be made in China, Vietnam, Bangladesh, or wherever the next low-price frontier develops.

9

Steep Learning Curves

The manufacturing company we owned was American Furniture Craftsmen. We made high-quality, casual, solid-oak tables and chairs. We sold our line to several leading retailers across the country, such as Nebraska Furniture Mart, Homemakers, Kacey's, Steinhafel's, and of course Schneiderman's. But manufacturing was a sideline for us, not our focus. I was motivated to start the company to create jobs in the little town of Meadowlands. At one point, we had 35 full-time workers. My brother Phil was a key person in the operation until his issues with alcoholism surfaced.

I learned some painful lessons from a Baptist minister, whom I'll call Leland. One day I was in a nearby town and I saw church furniture on display in a mall. It was well built. I noticed a brochure on one of the pews and tucked it into my pocket. It occurred to me that maybe I could use my knowledge of furniture and my contacts to open a manufacturing company in Meadowlands. I already had a building in mind and a dream when I called the phone number on the brochure. Leland was excited about my phone call and wanted to set up a meeting immediately. I needed Russell's support for the idea, so he and I drove up there along with our Meadowlands store manager to meet with Leland and his partner, Billy. In the meeting Leland went on and on, doing a lot of bragging. Talk, talk, talk. (My dad would have hated him.) One of the pieces he wanted to show us was a kneeler. He expounded on the wide-open market and huge need for kneelers because people want them for their bedrooms. Russ surprised me a little when he interrupted with, "For what, begging?"

Later that day, Russ, and I agreed Leland was likely full of you-know-what, but Russ said going forward was fine with him if I wanted to. We did suspect they were in some financial trouble. In time, we would find out he'd never actually sold any of his furniture in any significant sense.

Soon, I found out that the market for church furnishings is controlled by two or three manufacturers that dominate the business. They are low-cost, high-quality producers. A few basic calculations demonstrated there was no way we could compete, so we changed courses. Though my new partners were disappointed, I decided we would produce dining furniture. While they knew little about church furnishings, they knew nothing at all about residential furniture. Nevertheless, we plowed forward with starting the factory, hoping things would work out.

As we began to set up the factory and bring in equipment, it became apparent my new partners knew next to nothing about manufacturing. Further, they tended to move slow and procrastinate. Bob Anderson, who became the plant manager, picked up the slack.

One of the things Leland did that drove people up a wall was spout Bible verses in response to issues in the plant he disagreed with. One day after such an episode, Bob asked me to look up a specific verse. After I teased Bob about not having a Bible handy, I checked it out. Low and behold, the Word had been seriously misquoted.

Several months passed before we finally hired our initial group of employees and manufactured our first furniture. This was new to me and I was proud of the quality. It was rewarding.

Billy proved himself a craftsman who did quality work and fit in as part of the team. However, Leland spent most of his time talking and that got him into trouble with others. He had a know-it-all attitude that could be inappropriate. One day one of the workers was commenting on break about his paycheck being a little better thanks to some overtime. Leland took his own check out of his pocket, showed it to the worker, and said, "I wouldn't even show up if that's what I was paid."

When I got a call from Bob about the incident, oh, was I steamed. I went over there and asked Leland, "What in the world were you thinking? Why would you do such a thing?" I must have been carrying some additional passive aggression toward him because I added, "And, by the way, the Bible verse you cited the other day turns out to be a lie." Whoa, I surprised myself.

Later, I remember telling the pastor of my church while we were golfing, "I was a sucker for Leland because my mother has a tremendous respect for clergy that rubbed off on me. I just didn't do my normal amount of checking. I assumed he would be truthful."

"Didn't you say he was a Baptist?" the pastor asked. "You should know you can never believe a Baptist," he quipped. He was joking, of course, but I really should have done some due diligence. I think I wanted it to work so much that I didn't dig too deep.

Later, I wound up in arbitration with Leland. During the proceedings, he had to admit to making several false statements verbally and on his resume. The judge ruled in our favor. Billy remained with us. Once Leland was gone, we started losing less money and eventually turned a profit.

One of the keys to making a quality piece of furniture is the sanding process. If it's done consistently and well, the piece will not only look great, but feel great to the touch. At the plant, we had three men who did nothing but work with orbital sanders on the line all day. Unfortunately, a worker's compensation situation developed, which led Bob Anderson to suggest, "We need to give the guys more breaks with those things. They should have a job rotation to minimize strain."

"How's that going to impact the efficiency of the line?" I asked.

"We'll have to figure it out," Bob insisted. "Have you ever tried using one of those things, Larry?"

I admitted that, no, I hadn't.

"Why don't you come here after work and I'll show you what it's about."

I went over to the plant at about 5:00 that afternoon. The orbital sander is pretty heavy and after you do it for about 10 minutes—I'll tell you what, 10 minutes after you've put it down, you're still shaking from the vibration. I asked Bob to come up with a plan to rotate line workers to limit the time spent on the sander. "I already have a plan," he told me. "We'll start Monday."

As we discussed his rotation plan, I asked Bob something completely unrelated. "Do you think we should hire somebody to do what Leland was supposed to do?" He said he'd think about it.

A few days later, I got a letter from Sean Baaken, a young man working in our factory, that said, "Even though I'm doing sanding and I like my job, you don't know my background. I would like the chance to become the office manager." Though he was young and inexperienced, Sean proved to have great business sense, impressive work ethics, and natural customer service skills. Like Bob, he was committed to learning the business and succeeding. The other workers, happy to see Leland gone, were motivated to help Sean succeed. Sean and Bob were an excellent team and soon American Furniture Craftsmen started to meet its goals.

Looking back, I am amazed at how much the products were connected to Bob Anderson. He was incredibly talented and dedicated to what he was doing, but he had some personal struggles that resulted in panic attacks. He had to leave the company and I hired someone else who did a nice job, but was no Bob Anderson. By this time, Phil was also no longer involved in the company, and I had decided to relocate my family to the Twin Cities to be closer to our main furniture business. Russ and I sold American Furniture Craftsmen to a man who owned a wood-working business in a neighboring town. By the time we sold the business, it was profitable. We had some real leaders at the factory and they tried to help the new owner, but he wouldn't listen. He wreaked havoc with the employees and did nothing to grow the line. Ultimately, he went bankrupt.

I've always loved the furniture business. But I can't imagine any job exists that's free of some necessary but disagreeable task. For me, without question, that unappealing task was pursuing and collecting from those who didn't pay. I was responsible for managing the accounts receivable and following up on any delinquent accounts. In hindsight, it is obvious I should have put the brakes on the situation earlier, but we were so anxious to sell and make new customers that we didn't even want to check them out.

Today when you purchase from Schneiderman's, or any other furniture store, you use credit cards, checks, or financing. We don't extend credit. Any type of credit you get through a finance company is nonrecourse, which means if the customer defaults, the debt does not go back to the retailer. That's not the way things were years ago—prior to credit cards. In the past, a customer would come in to buy furniture or, worse yet, appliances (for whatever reason we had more problems with appliances, electronics, and televisions than with furniture) and we would give them credit. I'm sure some smart furniture stores checked a potential customer's credit beforehand, but we had never established that practice.

In Meadowlands, we were lucky in a way that people had to come so far to the store. Customers who had difficulty with credit were less likely to make such a long trip. We had few problems for many years. But when our business started to expand, the situation changed. Word got out among certain people and families that they could get credit at Schneiderman's, even if they weren't credit worthy. I recall one family in particular in which six members made an individual purchase from us. Of the six, I think only one paid his bill. The only reason he paid his bill is that we had gotten a bank contract and as part of the contract, he purchased life insurance. He died, so we got paid. The rest of the family never paid. Situations like these made extending credit pretty disagreeable. It felt personal when customers did not pay for the furniture they'd taken home and were using. It's like people stealing from you.

I would make a collection call if a customer had made a purchase six to seven months previous and hadn't paid. Fairly often they'd say things like, "It has a spring in it that makes a noise. That's why we aren't paying you." But they hadn't called to tell us there was a problem. I always loved to hear a response like that because then I'd say we would pick it up on Thursday and take care of the problem. And that's what we'd do—pick up the "problem" item, address whatever issue the customer claimed, then we'd call back and tell them we'd return after they paid. That scenario was an early lesson I learned from my dad.

We had a customer from Floodwood once who hadn't paid

for a La-Z-Boy recliner. I called him up and he said, "Well, we're not going to pay for it. It's defective. We told your dad about it."

"Then we'll pick it up and fix it." And I told my dad about the call.

"That's bullshit," he said. "But I'll tell you what. Fix it for them, but don't send it back to them until they pay."

Sadly, I guess I believed the customer more than my dad. We fixed the chair and brought it back, but he never paid us. That was a good lesson, and Dad's approach became my blueprint for how to handle similar situations. If people didn't pay their bills, we would go out of the way to work out accommodations with them. It's when they would lie and not pay us anything that we were forced into the repossession game.

Elizabeth Gordon is probably my favorite repossession story. She bought a whole bunch of furniture and appliances from us—a washer, dryer, refrigerator, microwave, mattress, box spring, TV, sofa, loveseat, and two recliners—and then just disappeared. She owed between $7,000 and $8,000, which was a big hit for us. In the Duluth-Superior area, we used a repair company, Gartner Appliance Repair, to service our appliances. One day, June Morse, who was still working at Schneiderman's in 2013, received a call from them. "We need a purchase date for a washer for a customer, Elizabeth Gordon, for a warranty claim."

We were still a small store with only a handful of employees, so June recognized the name immediately. "I think Larry's going to want to talk with you," she told the caller.

I called Gartner, requested Elizabeth Gordon's contact information, and indicated we'd take care of it from here.

"What do you mean?" Gartner asked. "Are you servicing now?"

"No," I told him. "She never paid for her purchase. We've been looking for her."

So June called Elizabeth Gordon and asked, "Is this Mrs. Gordon?"

"Who is this calling, please?" she asked.

"This is Gartner Appliance," June told her.

"This is she." Bingo. June set up a time to service her washer.

Russ and Bernie Dahl went to her house. Russ called me later that day and he said kiddingly, "There's good news and bad news."

"So what's the good news?"

"Well, we got to Gordon's and picked the stuff up."

"What could possibly be the bad news?"

It turned out the king-size mattress, box spring, and the TV weren't there, but she told them they could find those items at her brother's house. Russ asked what I thought they should do.

"Well, go get them."

"I was afraid you were going to say that."

As Russ tells the story, he arrived at the house and there were some men drinking in the middle of the afternoon watching *our* TV. Russ announced, "We're from Schneiderman's and we're here to pick up the mattress and the TV."

One of the men said, "I suppose you won't even let us watch the rest of the show."

Another joined in with, "I suppose you wouldn't take a bad check." Russ just unplugged the TV and he and Bernie carried it off.

Another appliance situation happened in Kinney, Minnesota. For whatever reason, that little town had a bunch of delinquent customers. One person stands out. He said he wasn't going to pay us for his refrigerator until we fixed the damn thing; he claimed it wasn't working. That's the first we'd heard of it. We could tell by his evasiveness and his attitude he wasn't going to pay us for it. So Russ went to his house. No one was home, but the door was open. Russ found out in a hurry why the refrigerator didn't work: They had no power. He wheeled the fridge out. When he got back to the store we were high-fiving ourselves that we got it back. Then I noticed Russ's pants were torn and his leg was bleeding. He had gone through a rotten board in the guy's porch on the way out.

We did everything we could to avoid repossessions. If people were upfront with us, we would go along with almost any payment plan.

We couldn't send our regular delivery drivers to repossess because they basically felt they weren't paid for that. It's a nasty business, but it was sometimes necessary. Whenever we did need to repossess, we left a signed note saying we would hold the furniture in our warehouse for 90 days pending payment arrangements, at which time we would bring the item back without delivery charges. If they didn't come through, we'd have to sell it. By the time most people got to this point of delinquency, let's face it—what's the stuff worth? Not much.

We developed an arrangement with the Floodwood Bank to finance through them. The bank would either approve or deny credit. If they did and the customer didn't pay, Schneiderman's was off the hook. My contact at the bank, Verna Furiel, was easy to work with. We often joked that we should write a book with the excuses we got for people being delinquent.

I had a customer right near Meadowlands who bought a dinette set from us. I called him and told him we were going to have to pick up the set unless he sent in a payment—it had been months and he had only paid $20. "Until the pigs get farrowed, it's out of the question," he told me.

I had no idea what that even was. I'm still not sure what it means. So I asked, "When will that be?"

Finally, I told him we would give him until September, but we wouldn't wait any longer.

Soon after, as I was talking to Verna at the bank on some

unrelated matters, I said, "By the way, Verna, I think I have a new excuse for our book. A customer told me I'd have to wait for his pigs to be farrowed."

Without waiting a beat, she said, "Leon Newburg owes *you* money too?" Apparently that was Leon's standard excuse for not paying his bills.

Once Russ and I had another customer who disappeared on us. We found out he lived on Highway 96, somewhere near Shoreview. We were planning to drive down to the furniture market in Minneapolis, so we decided we would see if we could locate him and pick up the recliner. The guy was belligerent and both Russ and I were a little concerned about how he might act. When we got there, a woman answered the door. We told her who we were and why we were there.

She let us in the house and we got the recliner, but we had a heck of a time getting it in my brother's Lincoln. We really wanted to get out of there before her husband came home. We were trying everything to get the chair loaded. The only way we could get the thing in the back seat was by leaving a window open. So, there we were in Minneapolis for three days with a recliner in our back seat and a window we couldn't close.

Another time, a customer had bought a 19" color TV from us. Without paying, he simply vanished from sight and we didn't hear from him again. Then one Saturday another customer came in, and for some reason the customer knew this guy hadn't paid for the TV. He gave us the address of a trailer park in Duluth. Sheila and I happened to be going out that night and it occurred to me that the trailer park was sort of along the way. I didn't share that information with my wife, of course, since she would have had the common sense to stop me. Without telling her why, I drove up to the place and saw this young man washing his Mustang. "George?" I asked.

"That's me. What can I do you for?"

(From left to right) Dad, me, Claudia, Phil, and Karen posing on our stoop just three years after Dad bought the general store. (1951)

Dad had carpentry skills that I do not possess, and always admired. Here he put them to good use and built a sandbox for Russ and me (left). (1952)

(From front to back) Russ, me, and our cousin Tom Toftey playing a summer baseball game with the Elmer Depot as our backstop. (1960)

The original Elmer general store (1948) juxtaposed against our newly remodeled Woodbury location (2014) is a testament to how far Schneiderman's has come. It's hard to imagine that, at one time, eight of us lived upstairs!

Why pink? Because the pink paint was cheap, that's why! (1958)

Mom loved to spend time talking with us in the garden (I think that day she was expounding on the Syrian Crisis). Not bad for 100! (2012)

Me and my son, Jason, at the grand opening of the Woodbury location. Every time we expand we want it to be better than the time before (mission accomplished). (2014)

"Most furniture stores will do anything to get you in the door. Not me."

"When I started selling furniture, people said I'd go out of business if I didn't have a sale once in awhile. That was 37 years ago. But some people still don't get it.

"Like the day I decided to run this ad. I called the newspaper and told the man I wanted four pages to advertise some of my furniture. The first thing he said to me was, 'You must be having a pretty big sale.'

"For the last time, I don't have sales. I don't have discounts (unless the manufacturer gives one to me). And I don't haggle with you. I make just one promise: to give you my absolute bottom price on furniture from the best manufacturers around. People like Thomasville, Flexsteel, Stiffel, and Stearns & Foster. And so far I've done pretty well.

"Take my word for it, the guys in my business know what they need to make a profit. And the price they set is going to do the job. No matter what they say about discounts and sale prices.

"But if you don't want to take my word for it, that's okay too. Just look at my prices on the next three pages. You'll see. Even though I don't use the gimmicks other furniture stores do, I sure know how to sell good furniture for less than the so-called discounters.

"And I've got 37 years of experi

Max Schneiderman

Schneiderman's

Dad was Schneiderman's spokesman in the mid-eighties, and had a firm stance on sales—"no sales" was one of his three core beliefs. (1985)

Dad was eventually overruled—and we had our first clearance sale. Even though he was a good sport and posed for the ad, rest assured that I suffered his silent treatment. (1986)

"3 out of 4 of us Schneidermans think a clearance sale is a good idea."

"Last year we talked dad into his first sale in 38 years of business. We pointed out that we'd overbought a few styles and had accumulated a lot of floor samples, discontinued one-of-a-kind pieces that we didn't know what to do with, and that we ought to have a clearance sale. Dad said we'd all lose our credibility if we had a sale, but we were free to make our own mistakes.

"Well, we had the sale and sold everything out and made a lot of folks happy. Now we're going to have another clearance sale for the same reasons May 9 & 10. But preferred customers like you can take advantage of the savings even earlier. Just come in Thursday or Friday May 7 & 8 before the sale starts and you'll have your choice of select styles of quality furniture, bedding and carpeting. We'll be open 'til 9:00 both those nights.

"Dad still doesn't think a clearance sale is a good idea, but he thinks it's more important we Schneidermans stick together when it comes to policy. That's why he agreed to help us with this sale. Thanks, dad."

Mom, Russell and Larry Schneiderman

Financing Available/Free Delivery
MasterCard/Visa Accepted/All Sales Final

P.S. There's another sale going on in our store during our Clearance Sale. This sale is being put on by Sealy and they're offering instant cash rebates of up to $75 on their mattresses. How nice of Sealy to make our everyday low prices even lower.

Duluth (Hwy. 53 across from Target): 218/723-2302
Lakeville (Take Hwy. 50 to downtown): 612/469-3900
Meadowlands (Just outside of town): 218/427-2118

Schneiderman's

(From left to right) Molly, Russ, Monica, and John at Russ' retirement party. Russ was known for his prominent mustache, so we sported mustaches in solidarity. (December 2008)

I always looked forward to "working" with Harry Bassett at the furniture markets. He brought a lot of fun to the business and has been missed since his passing in 2012. (2010)

Russ loved the Twins, and had a part-time job in security. The day after his death, the Minnesota Twins honored him with a moment of silence and his picture on the scoreboard. (August 2011)

My mom and my brother Phil. Phil was, without a doubt, one of the most intelligent people I've ever known. He died July 30, 2010, and I miss our conversations.

Jason and his wife, Natalie, enjoying some time off at Block Island. But don't be misled—he'll be checking his emails later. (2002)

Me and Jenna at Block Island. There are family vacations you reminisce about, and this trip is one of them. Over a decade later, and we're still talking about it. What a place; what a time.

(From left to right) John, Monica, and Molly Schneiderman. Russ was a family man, first and foremost. (March 2012)

David taking a joyride with John at the 2010 Kretzschmar Reunion.

Sheila with our first grandchild, Quinn. She was worth the wait! (2014)

Our grandmother, Josephine Kretzschmar, a strong, intelligent, and faithful woman who raised six exceptional children.

(From left to right) Russ, Karen, me, Claudia, and Mom at the 2010 Kretzschmar Reunion... with Bob Braun photobombing in the background. Every four years, about 100–125 Kretzschmars gather to congratulate each other on our great gene pool.

(From left to right) Chris, Jodi, Jenna, and Collin celebrating darn good furniture and Christmas. (2013)

(From left to right) Me, Sheila, Natalie, Jodi, Chris, and Jason on a Mississippi River cruise. You rarely will hear me say "always," but I always appreciate spending time with my family. (2013)

Jodi and Chris in China getting to know their daughter, Quinn. (February 2013)

The family showing off the Kretzschmar family crest.
Mom was proud of the turnout, but she shouldn't have
been surprised. (July 2010)

"You can get my TV. I'm Larry Schneiderman."

"Oh go f—yourself."

I heard the unmistakable sound of Sheila locking the doors of our car. Despite George's less-than-cordial greeting, I went inside and took the TV. I was half expecting him to turn the hose on me or worse, but he didn't.

In hindsight, I think we took delinquent or non-payments too personally. It became a personal trust issue to us. Instead of agonizing over the symptoms, I should have put a halt to the cause sooner. Dealing with the small minority of people who try to avoid paying their bills can sour a person on people in general. I'm glad that nobody at Schneiderman's has to deal with the issue these days.

Today, we have a disciplined hiring process that usually involves multiple interviews as well as testing and background checks. It wasn't that way at the beginning, yet still, from time to time, we hire someone who just isn't right for Schneiderman's.

When we first started hiring for sales consultants, Dad was retired and Mom was working weekends only. She stopped selling when we computerized. She had no interest in technology. Up until then, though she was in her seventies, she'd only been thinking about retiring from the sales floor. Nonetheless, she continued to help us in other ways in later years. Another factor for her retirement was that Schneiderman's was using a sales commission system for compensating our salespeople. That made her uncomfortable because she worried she was depriving others from making a living.

My dad used to joke (darkly) that there are two things wrong with the furniture business—customers and employees. I suppose his gallows humor is true in the sense that our success relies on our relationships with our employees and the ongoing goodwill of our customers. Those two vital and complex sets of human relationships are our biggest ongoing challenge and the sources of our greatest rewards. Some of the repossession stories above demonstrate some of the customer side of Dad's assessment. I've also had some unfortunate experiences with employee stories that illustrate the other side. Often it was a case of—as they say—too smart, too late.

The first person I hired earned a place in my hall of fame of poor choices. He was a young, good-looking guy who had just completed a two-year design program at White Bear Lake Technical College. I remember telling my wife that I thought women would like him. And they often did. Too much.

He and his wife initially enjoyed living in Meadowlands, but ultimately began to go stir-crazy. There aren't many secrets in a small town, and he was creating a lot of interest between his drinking and his behavior. One night, a friend of mine was in a local bar and the owner heard what he thought was a radio playing in the restroom. This annoyed him, because he wanted people to use his jukebox. So he headed to the bathroom to put a stop to it. There was my star salesman sitting on the toilet playing the harmonica. "Virgil," he said, "the acoustics in here are something else." So was he.

His behavior became worse, and quickly. He was immature, a womanizer, and likely an alcoholic. Eventually, his partner threw rocks to break all the windows in the place they were renting. Then she left town. Just as I was about to terminate him, he left town as well.

I wanted to learn from that situation. I wanted somebody solid, hopefully a non-drinker for starters. I hired a young man who was as nice and solid as they come, but who didn't have any sales experience. I noticed he kept an index card in his pocket each day. One day I asked him what was on it, and he said he used the cards to memorize Bible verses. Everything about him was authentic and believable, but he couldn't sell a piece of furniture if his life depended on it. I didn't know what to do about him. I liked him a lot, but he wasn't accomplishing his job. One day he told me, "I hate to do this to you. I'll stay as long as you want, but I've been accepted into the ministry." I was so happy for him. And for me.

Next I hired someone with sales experience; I thought that's where I'd gone wrong with my previous hire. This guy didn't have any experience selling furniture, but he had been on a truck route selling meat. He was also a nice guy. My dad would come around the store regularly to have a cup of coffee with me, and every time he saw the new sales guy he'd ask, "When are you getting rid of him? He can't sell furniture."

"Give him a chance," I'd say. "We're working with him."

So, one day the sales guy is working with two women in the store. One of the women asked, "Will this sofa go with my carpeting?"

"I don't know, but ask me anything about a wiener or a steak and I'll tell you." The two women just looked at each other. I realized I had no choice but to take action. My dad even told me he wouldn't come into the store until the guy was gone. Ultimately he had to go, so I finally took action.

It was difficult getting people to live in Meadowlands, but finally I found a salesman who seemed like he would be the right fit. He was in his early thirties, and had worked for a car dealership. I called the owner of the dealership and asked what they knew about him. They told me he was their top salesman. As an added bonus, he had a good background in furniture. So, I hired him as selling manager at the store.

Soon it became clear that his view of sales practices was different than mine. He would charge different people different prices for the same piece of furniture. He had his rationale for this, and there's no law against it. After years of learning from my dad, though, I regarded it as wrong, much to his frustration. He also had a tendency to not listen to customers, particularly if they had a service issue. In addition, alcohol was beginning to play a problematic role in his life. I had heard he liked to hang out at the local bars, and he frequently came into work talking about being hungover. He was a manager, and I expected him to be a role model for our other employees. I discussed the issue with him in private, focusing more on his work-day boasts about being hungover than anything else. What he did in private was up to him, but I needed to remind him he was a reflection of our store. These differences accumulated to create a wider and wider gulf between us.

Then a friend who also knew the car dealer the manager had worked for previously told me, "He's a sharp guy, but he's someone who would rather make $100 dishonestly, than $200 honestly. It is just the way he is." Looking back, I realize that I bore a share of responsibility for the whole situation. I was looking for an aggressive manager and salesperson, and I didn't dig as deeply as I should have. Finally I told him he wasn't working out as a manager, but he's a heck of a salesperson and if he'd abide by the rules, I wanted him to stay on in that role. Given his selling skills, his income would likely increase if he focused exclusively on sales. I thought if he didn't need to make management decisions, he'd be a helpful contributor to our team. But hard feelings are inevitable when a pay decrease or demotion is involved—which isn't an unreasonable reaction. He continued in a sales role for two more years and performed fairly well. From time to time, though, his negative feelings would surface and create a challenge for his manager.

If a person doesn't perform to expectations, to place them in a lower-paying or otherwise diminished position may seem a reasonable strategy, or at least a kindness, but it doesn't work. The employee will inevitably harbor hard feelings. Good intentions on the employer side aren't enough. I should have learned that lesson from this initial mistake, but I was destined to repeat similar scenarios twice more in my career.

One of the smartest people who ever worked for me wanted more and more authority. But she exhibited a bulldozer personality that resembled Phil's in some ways. People just couldn't work with her. Eventually it got to the point that when I had to meet with her, I'd get a stomachache. Her intensity created that much stress around her. I would try to word things carefully, but anytime someone disagreed with her, including me, a battle ensued. Since she held a key position in the company, it was a complicated separation. Several months after she left the company, one employee told me that sometimes he would still drive around the building just to make sure he wasn't only dreaming she was gone. In retrospect, I know that I had been intimidated by her as well. I should have taken some of the comments I had heard about her over the years more seriously. It's difficult to measure what the situation cost us in terms of morale. Addressing the problem was my responsibility and I dragged my feet in getting it done.

Once I had a rare opportunity to speak with one of the most successful businesspeople I've ever known. I asked him, "Ed, if you could go back and do things differently, is there anything you would change?"

He thought for a bit and then offered, "I would have fired more people." That seemed like a surprising statement. He went on to explain that when an individual is a bad fit for a specific position or for a company, it's actually a kindness to cut the string. It protects the company, and gives the employee an opportunity to seek a position at another company that may suit him or her better.

Some years later, I was at a conference with perhaps businesspeople and the facilitator asked how many of us had fired someone. Nearly every hand went up. "Now," he continued, "how many of you regret firing those people?" Not one hand went up.

An experienced consultant once told me he could diagnose which companies were too slow to make necessary personnel changes by asking one question: "Have you ever heard management say after an employee leaves, 'This is a good thing.'" If so, the company waited too long before taking the necessary action. Strong, healthy companies don't wait for an employee who is a poor fit to leave on their own.

Every so often, somebody in our performance group will mention a plan to terminate an employee. I'll make a note of it and ask at the next meeting how the firing went. In almost all cases, they haven't gone through with it. Why? Well, it's a life-changing event that no one should take lightly. But on top of that, we often wonder if we'll be able to find somebody better.

There are other complications that keep us challenged. Workers' compensation insurance rates seem to be on a continual rise. Sometimes those claims are complicated to manage, especially in those few cases in which an employee may misrepresent their injury.

There are also times an employee may need to be fired for misconduct. That was the case with three sales consultants at one of our showrooms who were drinking alcohol at work. We fired all three of them for misconduct and none received unemployment, but two felt they were entitled to it. For some reason, many people don't understand how unemployment works. Many seem to believe they have already paid for this somehow. They either don't understand, or don't care, that the employer pays for it all. We are careful about protesting a person's unemployment claim because it can create hard feelings. My first experience with this was up in Meadowlands, early in my career. A driver's assistant quit without any advance notice to take a higher-paying job in construction. He was laid off a week later and filed for unemployment. We had correctly classified his status as "employee quit," which would disqualify him for unemployment coverage based on his time with us. I ran into the former employee's dad who told me he was really "pissed" at us because we "took away his kid's unemployment." No amount of explaining could make him feel better.

What's so unfortunate about negative experiences with customers or employees is how these experiences loom so much larger than all the good ones happening throughout each day. Sadly, the negative stories get told and retold more often than the positive ones. Sometimes policies are initiated to manage a very small percentage of difficult people. In some cases, no-win situations have their roots in our own mistakes—and occasionally the only positive outcome is the lesson learned.

10

Jason, Jodi, and Jenna

My son, Jason, has a learning disability, and we had some challenges with him. Sheila and I look back and have some regrets about how we parented him. When we married, I was 21 and she was 20. We were married less than three years when Jason was born, so we were awfully young. Growing up in a town as small as Meadowlands was a detriment to Jason because of our visibility. He did poorly in school and a lot of that manifested into behavior issues. I remember how much we hated going to teacher conferences. I remember his second-grade teacher telling us all the things he was doing, and not doing.

"I don't know what you're going to do," she said. She looked up and she realized we were pretty devastated. She put her hand on my arm and she said, "You know, Mr. Schneiderman, he isn't the worst in the class." I think our expectations of him were pretty high.

In the fourth grade, Jason had a teacher named Jim Ohman who had earned a reputation for being an especially effective teacher. Everybody liked Jim, and we thought he was great. As we left a conference with him, Jim said, "I've had a lot of boys like Jason over the years and here's what I'm going to tell you. I'm going to be blunt. He's never going to do well in school, but he's going to be great in life. He's going to be fine when he's, say, about 22."

As we left the school, Sheila turned to me and said, "That's 10 more years!"

Jason had what was called a strong "word attack." If I asked him to read aloud to me, he did well. You wouldn't guess anything was wrong at all. The problem was that he couldn't comprehend or repeat back what he had just read. Sheila and I devised all sorts of rewards to encourage him to tell us what he had read, but he just couldn't do it. Moving along through the elementary grades and beyond was tough for him, and it became even tougher. I'm told schools have improved their capacity to help students with learning disabilities. Actually, I read about some interesting recent studies concerning dyslexics. The December 12, 2007, issue of *Bloomberg Businessweek* quoted Dr. Sally Shagwitz of Yale University: "Many of the coping skills dyslexics learn in their formative years become best practices for a successful entrepreneur. Being a slow reader forces you to extract only vital information, so you're constantly getting to the important points."

So, it's easy to imagine that when Jason was assigned to read *Grapes of Wrath* as an eighth grader, it was the mother of all impossible assignments. In this particular case, Jason would fail the course if he didn't get a passing grade on the book test. I hadn't read the book, so I offered to Jason to read some every night with him as long as he agreed to give me his full attention. I think we both came to enjoy that nightly activity. The teacher expressed amazement when Jason got an "A" on the test. That was a memorable moment.

His learning disability carried over to all subjects. I remember working with him on the multiplication tables. We would do a couple each night. Over and over, we would work on, for instance, 8 x 1 = 8, 8 x 2 = 16, and so on. One night he was particularly frustrated and he blurted out to me, "Dad, it won't do any good, anyway. My teacher says we're moving on to division next week." I just thought, oh boy. . . how will he keep up?

Jason started smoking when he was 16. We know he was drinking alcohol as well. It wasn't unusual for kids to drink up there, but we were afraid Jason had chemical issues because there's a history of alcoholism in both our families. He tried college for a while, but it didn't work for him. For awhile he really struggled with what he wanted to do. He told me he wanted to go to work for us. I told him I didn't think it was a good idea. "You need to find something on your own for at least a year, then we can talk about it."

Given his state at the time, I thought he needed to work some on his own rather than wind up at Schneiderman's by default. He needed to bring some skills and experience outside the family business with him. I think it may have been one of the best decisions I've ever made. But in the moment, it was a tough one.

Jason wound up going to work for a furniture finisher and repair expert. He did well there and later came to work at our distribution center, where he was part of a three-man crew working the second shift. My brother Phil was working for us at the Lakeville store then and Jason impressed him. "Your kid has fire in his gut," he told me one day.

In those days, Jason wasn't listening to me much and I was grateful Phil took him under his wing. I was a little nervous given Phil's personal struggles, yes, but grateful.

Jason was impressing people with how hard he was working in the warehouse. He had knowledge others didn't for difficult furniture repairs. I was hearing positive comments about his work. Phil suggested Jason take some Dale Carnegie courses. Carnegie started teaching adults leadership courses in 1912; since then they've evolved into global leadership-based training. I thought it was a good idea, but at the time, Jason wasn't interested. As a consolation, he told Phil he would *think* about it. I told Jason we'd gladly pay for the courses, and finally he agreed. I don't want to say these courses changed who he was, but it woke something up in him. At his final class session, I was invited to attend and listen to his speech. I was so proud; I remember thinking maybe it would all work out for Jason after all.

He took a sales consultant position in the Lakeville store. I started hearing from him in the evenings when he'd call to talk about his daily experiences. Later, he became the assistant store manager at Lakeville, working with Mikki Morin. When we opened up an outlet store in Chaska, he became the selling manager. Though the store was smaller, with only three or four employees, he gained valuable experience being responsible and accountable.

We ended up closing the outlet store after determining it had been a mistake to open an outlet store in Chaska, which was too far away from our distribution center in Lakeville. The store wasn't a financial disaster; it just didn't make good business sense to have something out so far.

While things went well for Jason as a selling manager, he was anxious to put his own ideas into play. He got the opportunity to do so when we opened our new store at Maple Grove in 2000. At the time, the location was a real gem. The store was built during the turbulent Thomasville time. Russ and I had planned it as a Thomasville prototype before we decided to go as strictly Schneiderman's. The store was laid out in an open-display manner that's more typical today than it was then. Jason hired the staff and proved himself a capable manager. What a pleasure it was to visit the store occasionally and go to lunch with him.

When we closed the Maple Grove store in 2006 to open our largest showroom in Plymouth, Jason became store manager there. While the Maple Grove showroom impressed people, the new Plymouth location was three times bigger and so were its challenges. Plymouth became our number-one store right away and remains so, at least into 2013.

For several years, Russ expressed frustration that he wanted to retire, but didn't see how that would be possible. I don't remember what the specific issue was, but one day we were disagreeing on some point and he said, "Why don't you buy me out?" It shocked me, though it shouldn't have because I knew he was getting tired of the demands of the business. I shot him a look, and he looked back at me, as if to say, "Damn it, I mean it."

The next day, we went to lunch and I told him that if he was serious, maybe, there's a way, but let's not do it in anger.

"I'm not angry," he told me. "I'd just like to do something else, and I don't see how it will happen." I think a key to our relationship was that being brothers trumped being business partners. So in 2008 we did find a way and Russ was happy about it. He took on a dream job for him, working in security for the Minnesota Twins. They were good to him and he loved the job.

When Russ left, Jason assumed several of his responsibilities for buying. Jason works with Susan Strong, our merchandise manager, and his wife, Natalie Stob, who purchases accessories. I think our buying team does a great job. Jason has also assumed responsibility for our advertising, which is an important and time-consuming responsibility. In my opinion, right from the start, we've had one of the best websites in our market. Since Jason has assumed overall responsibility, he's been implementing some excellent site innovations that are making it even better.

Jason knows I mean it as a "dark compliment" when I sometimes call him Phil. I'm extremely proud of the fact he quit smoking, a habit he had for maybe 20 years, and lost weight by working out.

He's extremely passionate about the business. We talk nearly every night on the phone, whether I feel like it or not. He tells me about the events of the day. At about the time I'm winding down for the night, he wants to discuss his latest idea. One of the characteristics I appreciate most about him is that he's a learner. Like many younger people, he embraces technology. The furniture industry is not known for leading the way in technology, but Schneiderman's has always made every effort to utilize new technology. Having a leader like Jason who embraces growth in technology only makes us stronger. In some ways our styles are different, but he will do well. His mind will still be on business even when he's not at the store. It's kind of the way I am. Natalie, Jason's wife, is the same way, which helps make them a good match.

I think most parents who own businesses and love what they're doing dream about all their kids working with them and everyone living happily ever after. The idea of keeping your kids close and working with them every day seems like a dream come true. But, so often, it turns to heartache. I know many people in family businesses and if they're being candid, they'll admit that being in business together often creates issues among them that can become deep and personal. Multiple siblings have different abilities and work ethics. It's not unusual for siblings' partners to become involved as well. Over the years, I've shared many conversations with people running family businesses. Overall, I'd say more conflicts in family dynamics are created than are solved as the result of family members being in business together.

Russ and I were brothers first. We certainly didn't agree with each other on every business issue or question. A successful consultant once commented to me, "If a company has partners who agree on everything, one of them is not needed." While we were different from each other in business style, having two Larrys or two Russells running Schneiderman's wouldn't have worked as well as one of each. While Jason and I challenge each other from time to time, we respect each other as business partners, but value our relationship above all else.

Jodi, my eldest daughter, is a lot like my mother in many ways, which means she's also a lot like me. We lived close to my mom's house while Jodi was growing up. When she would get frustrated with Sheila or me, she would run away to my mom's place, where she'd be told, "You can stay until after dinner, then you have to go home."

Jodi, unlike her brother, Jason, had no interest in the family business from early on. She was always strong and independent. I did try to involve her in the store, but she simply expressed no interest, or as she says, "You paid me lower wages than the non-family got for the same work." I don't remember that, but it sounds like something I would have done.

I wanted my kids to work in the store while they were in high school, and Jodi worked with competence, but she was bored with it and there was no mistaking that. To this day, we go back and forth about the rebellious attitude she had growing up. She's my opposite in some ways, even though we're pretty close. Sometimes I wonder if she might share my perspectives more often if she wasn't thinking: *Dad thinks this is so great. . . .* Maybe not.

Jodi could be exasperating in her teen years. She was very independent. We had to tell her, if you can't follow our rules, then find a new place to live. So, guess what? She didn't come home one Friday night. All night we worried and wondered where she was. It wasn't like her to do that sort of thing. Sheila knew her best friend, Kim, worked as a receptionist at our store on Saturday mornings. Sheila called Kim at the store and said, "We need to know where Jodi is. I know you know where she is." Finally, Kim told her.

I went to pick Jodi up and told her how worried we were.

"You told me, if I couldn't follow the rules then don't come home."

"You little pissant," I retorted. I don't even know why I said it, because it isn't an expression I use. She still throws that at me from time to time.

Jodi has earned two master's degrees, one in industrial organizational psychology, and another in counseling. After she completed graduate school, she got a job at Harley-Davidson in Milwaukee as a change management consultant. We were proud of her new job—not surprised, but proud. We were amazed by her starting salary and benefits there. Unfortunately, she discovered that she didn't care for the corporate world or Milwaukee.

We got a call from her one night and she said, "Are you sitting down?" Now, parents don't like to hear questions like that from a daughter. She'd had many boyfriends, so we held our breaths. It turned out that she planned to quit her job and move to Denver with her friends and former college roommates, Natalie and Angie, who also both had good jobs elsewhere in the country. Why Denver? Two reasons. It has the second most days of sunshine than anywhere else in the United States. (San Diego is number one, but they knew they couldn't afford San Diego, so they chose Denver.) Number two, it has a high population of single men. Sheila and I were upset—our first reaction was not positive. We thought she was nuts. And, in fact, that's what we told her. She came right back at me with, "Dad, what's all this drivel you're spouting about 'I Hope You Dance'?"

It's a Lee Ann Womack song that encourages people to not sit on the sidelines, to get out there and try, even if you fail. I kept telling her, this is the song for you, but now she wanted to take this incredible leap, and we said she was nuts. Anyway, next time we talked to her, we were more supportive, but after we hung up the phone, Sheila said, "I still think she's nuts."

It was a good move, though, because she met Chris out there and they're a great combination. They have a lot of fun together, traveling all over the world, hiking, camping, and loving Colorado. He will eventually be a professor. He's studying for his PhD right now. Jodi is a career counselor at a college in Boulder. In February 2014, Jodi and Chris adopted Quinn, our first grandchild, a beautiful two-year-old girl from China.

I have no doubt she could have been successful in a lot of ways in the furniture business, if she'd chosen to pursue it. When we hired a human resources person a couple years ago, I floated it by her because it matches her background and she would be great at it. But she loves Colorado. I would have liked to work with her, just as I enjoy working with Jason.

If it doesn't top the list of best choices Sheila and I ever made, adoption is certainly up there. When we lived near Meadowlands, before we had kids, two of the couples in our church adopted Korean children and we were drawn to those kids. We had an affinity for them and we said, "After we have a couple kids, let's adopt a Korean child." When you're young, you think and dream and say things without considering reality. Frequently, those dreams don't work out. Your life changes, you forget, or you find yourself no longer in the position to do what you wanted. But in this case, our early dream worked out. We had Jason and Jodi and then, even though Sheila has had rheumatoid arthritis since she was in her twenties, often making even simple tasks difficult, we wanted to adopt a Korean baby girl. Fortunately, at the time we were looking into the process seriously, Sheila's arthritis hadn't been as bad. We probably wouldn't have adopted otherwise.

Jenna was two-and-a-half months old when she arrived in Minnesota. The adoption agency we used was Lutheran Social Services (LSS) and as part of their process, we received helpful mandatory counseling. There were a lot of things we didn't know and many common adoption scenarios they were able to walk us through. Everybody is different, but there are certainly things everybody should and shouldn't do. Sheila and I went by the book.

As a child, when Jenna was sad she'd say, "I want my birth mother." Not her birth father, her birth mother. This is pretty common for adopted children.

The LSS counselor said a trip to Korea, if you could do it, with a group like Children's Home Society, is a wonderful thing, but the best age is when the child is 12. When they're younger than 12, the kids don't get as much out of it as they could, and teenagers are harder to handle. One of the most treasured memories I have—and I hope that's the case for Jenna too—is the trip the two of us made to Korea when she was 12.

When Jenna was younger and would get sad and want her birth mother, we would tell her, "When you're 12 we'll go to Korea and we'll try to find your birth mother." When she turned 12, we made plans to do it. Sadly, Sheila was in no condition for a trip like that, so Jenna and I went on our own. Before we went, I contacted Children's Home Society and said I would like, if at all possible, to locate Jenna's birth mother because I had promised Jenna we would do that. I was told that finding her was unlikely, but they promised to try their best. They were able to locate Jenna's birth mother, but she was afraid to see us because the present man in her life didn't know she'd had a child. A visit from a 12-year-old American daughter would put her in a real predicament. "I'm sorry," they said to me.

I knew a lot of other adoptive parents who had been in the same situation, so I knew what questions to ask. "Well, I'd like you to locate the birth mother's mother—Jenna's grandmother," I told my contact at Children's Home Society.

"Why is that?" she asked.

"If we can't meet Jenna's mother, I'd like her to try and meet her grandmother and maybe she could talk her daughter into meeting us."

"Well, Larry, that's kind of risky."

"I don't want to sound cold about this, but my first allegiance is to my daughter. I need her mother to know this is her one and only chance. Can you get that message to her? We will meet her anywhere; she doesn't have to come to Seoul. That might help."

We got to Korea and some of the kids met their birth mothers, but most of them didn't. It's devastating for the kids, and sad for the adults. One little girl who had become friends with Jenna on the trip couldn't stop crying no matter what we did to try and soothe her.

The trip was busy. We met the doctor who gave birth to Jenna. We went to the orphanage where she stayed, and were able to hold the other kids. They had set opportunities for the adopted children to experience South Korean culture. The children were able to eat local foods, wear traditional outfits, and participate in so many ways. It was a great cultural experience.

After several days in Seoul, I received a phone call and was told meeting Jenna's birth mother wasn't going to happen. Jenna was sad, but I think she expected this was probably going to happen based on what happened with these other girls.

But two days later I got a call at 6:00 a.m.: Jenna's biological mother had changed her mind. She agreed to see us if we traveled to Mokpo, a small fishing village in the western part of Korea. Jenna and I flew there with Mrs. Han, our social worker and interpreter. We met Jenna's mother at a past-its-prime hotel. She came with her little daughter, who I guess would be Jenna's half-sister.

Before the meeting, Jenna had asked me, "What should I say?"

"Honey, I have no idea, but it will come to you." This was

entirely new ground for both of us.

By coincidence, it was Jenna's mother's birthday the day we met her. So Jenna bought her some flowers and expressed through the interpreter, "Happy birthday." The woman didn't realize it was her birthday because they go by the lunar month, not the Julian calendar.

Her birth mother told her, "There has never been a day I haven't thought of you."

"I pray for you every day," Jenna said. It's rare for me to get tears in my eyes, but this was one of those occasions.

Korean birth mothers, we'd been told, often start feeling their birth daughter's faces. And it had turned out to be true in this case. Sheila had written down a number of questions for me to ask the mother, in part because we were wondering about any family history of health issues. We also knew nothing about Jenna's biological father—nothing. So we asked about him and how they met. She said they both worked for a garment factory in Seoul when she got pregnant. The two of them went to the supervisor's office and made him aware of the situation. The supervisor told the young man, "I want you to leave now, I never want to see you again, and I never want you to see her again." It was the last time she saw him.

My wife and I wanted to fund her education, but we were told by Lutheran Social Services that it wasn't a good idea. I asked the interpreter, who was also a social worker, "Does it ever happen in Korea that a woman gives birth out of wedlock, and then does well?"

She said never.

"No hope whatsoever? You can't tell me of one situation where a woman had a baby out of wedlock and later became happily married with a good job?"

"Never." It was the stigma of having a child out of wedlock. It may have changed by today; I hope it has. But Jenna is 26 now, so that was only 14 years ago.

At the end of our meeting, we all rode in a cab to the bus station where Jenna's birth mother and half-sister were to board a bus for their trip home and we were to board one to begin our journey back to Seoul. Jenna's birth mother hugged her and said "Thank you" to me through our interpreter. We climbed in our bus, where from our seats we could see them looking at us from inside the station.

"You know, you have time if you want to go and hug her one last time," I told Jenna.

Jenna left the bus and hugged her birth mother for the last time—likely ever. It was pretty sad. I couldn't hold back my tears, seeing Jenna and her birth mother holding each other. I couldn't help but think of how hard it must have been to give up such a beautiful daughter, and then see only briefly the beautiful woman she was growing up to be.

Jenna had the opportunity to continue to write her through the social worker. We told her, "We're not going to nag you. If you want to do it, it's totally up to you." She wrote once, but never received a response.

I think Jenna needed to satisfy the curiosity to meet her birth mother. She doesn't express everything that is going on in her thoughts, and her birth mother rarely comes up in conversation. We have pictures and movies of this whole thing, but I've never had her come home and say, "Dad, where are those pictures of Korea?" or anything like that. It's up to her.

Sometimes we talk about the great trip we had to Korea, though. I think we were fortunate—few daughters and fathers get to share that kind of thing. Those two weeks we spent in Korea were a tremendous bonding experience.

Jenna is artsy—and an accommodating, genuinely nice person. Being adopted, she's a bit of a contrast to the Schneiderman gene pool. At the age of six, she was already playing the piano. Someone once commented, "For a Schneiderman to have musical abilities you only had to go as far as Korea." Let's just say we are not, in general, a musically inclined family.

We were somewhat surprised when she got involved in sales at our Plymouth store. She is extremely gifted as a sales consultant. She knows the mechanics of selling and how to be involved with a customer to locate their needs, and she has good follow-up. During the time she was at the Plymouth store, she became one of our top sales consultants, which is unusual for such a young person. It was fun having her around. I know Jason and Natalie enjoyed working with her and were impressed with how she did. Jason would listen to her with customers when he could and commented, "I hope our training doesn't screw her up—she's a natural."

Jenna's husband, Collin, is from Burnsville. Both of them are graduates of the College of Visual Arts in St. Paul, and they're living in New York City. Collin is an extremely talented painter and illustrator. His illustrations, to my eye, are professional quality. He's a perfectionist in many ways—and I love that he makes the best carrot cake ever! They both love New York, as I imagine many young artists would. It's an expensive place to live, but they are both hard workers and they do well. Jenna talks about moving back sometime, and I hope she does, but that's up to them. We'd love to have her back in the business. That would really be helpful, but it is their decision.

11

What I've Learned

I find tremendous joy in the furniture business. I have a diffi-cult time thinking about a day I didn't enjoy for one reason or another.

When we train new sales consultants, we take them through a 10-day training course. During that time, we cover a lot of territory—from the nuts-and-bolts administrative information to sales training, product knowledge, and computer training. I also meet with the group to share a DVD about our company and respond to questions. Then I give each employee a simple booklet we go through together, "Things I've Learned from Others in the Furniture Business." Just because something is simple, doesn't make it easy. It's in the execution.

These are little things, common sense, but they're little things often not practiced. These lessons hold so much meaning for me because they're lessons I've learned through others, espe-cially my mom and dad.

1. Don't be afraid to say, "I don't know." *By acknowledging we don't know an answer and by taking immediate steps to find out, we build trust. The world is full of knowledgeable people. It's less full of people who care enough to admit they don't know the answer, but will find out. Honesty builds trust.*

It's especially difficult for a person lacking confidence to admit they don't know something. Confidence is an important attribute of an excellent sales consultant. But if a person isn't learning all the time, how will they grow in confidence? By asking questions and being sure of base knowledge, competence grows. Customers know when a person is guessing, or worse, trying to make up answers to questions they don't know anything about. From time to time, a personal friend will want me to help them pick out furniture. I don't know enough about our products anymore to be an effective consultant. Nonetheless, some good friends wanted me to help them pick out some family room furniture. Despite my plea, he wanted *me* to help them. I honestly didn't know what product was made by what company. My friends were looking at motion sofas and asked me why one was so much more than another, even though they looked the same. I jokingly stammered, "Stop trying to make me prove what I already told you." Meanwhile, his wife found the cord and pointed out to me that the more expensive motion sofa was electric, like car windows. "Ah, I see." We have so many brands, so many new products, and it takes more than sales skills to be effective. It takes an awareness of product changes that occur every single week. Luckily, my friends did buy from me, though I'm sure it was out of sympathy.

The Internet has made this even a bigger issue. Customers sometimes study a single product and they come into the store knowing more than we do. When they do, the only smart choice is to compliment them and, perhaps, be open to learning something from our customer. Ouch.

I've had factory reps make the same mistake. We were shopping for sofa-sleepers and the rep didn't think we were serious, so he guessed on prices. When we came back to buy, it became embarrassingly obvious he hadn't quoted the right prices. He made excuses about the price sheets being confusing and I asked, "Or, could it be you thought we were wasting your time and you guessed?" He was embarrassed. When he came clean, we bought anyway.

2. The eight-foot rule and its sidekick. *Never let a shopper pass within eight feet without smiling and welcoming. Here's its sidekick: Never fail to look up and acknowledge our shopper as she moves near you. If you're on the phone or gazing at a computer screen, stop, look up, and smile. Stop, look, and listen. . . . It's the safest way to happy customers.*

I am impressed when I'm at a business where the employees appear to be happy to be there. There were six of us at the BLVD Kitchen in Minnetonka on an Easter Sunday. Whoever hires people there has my admiration. To a person, they smiled, were helpful, and as I commented to my daughter-in-law, Natalie, they all exuded an attitude of, "I sure am glad to be working my butt off on Easter Sunday." We should be thankful people come to our stores, whether we're working with them or not. There's a lot of stress and unpleasantness in the world; let our place be a respite.

Don't walk by a customer or anyone without a welcoming smile, whether the smile is returned or not. Occasionally we have to remind our people to drop what they're doing when a customer is nearby. We need to acknowledge people, show them we know they're important. Customers sometimes signal their desire to be left alone by looking the other way and avoiding eye contact. Still, maintain the habit of smiling and saying "hello." They're our customers and can greet us in return or not, but we are charged with making their experience a good one.

3. The best open probe of all time is, "Tell me about your room." *Great sales consultants help people have beautiful rooms. It's far more rewarding than selling somebody a couch. Expressing sincere interest in her room will resonate with our shopper. "Tell me about your room" is not something a lesser sales consultant will ask. Sketching fits right in.*

We all hate to have somebody want to sell us something that isn't right or that we don't need. When we ask about the customer's room, and then listen carefully, we separate ourselves in a good way. We are trying to help. There is a great deal more satisfaction in helping a customer build a great room instead of just selling them a sofa. We have beautiful vignettes in our store and frequently a customer will buy just the sofa and really miss the potential. On the other hand, I've had customers tell me they've gone into a newly furnished room in their home and felt it was like a dream. That's what we love to do!

4. Handle the shopper with care. *We never know what kinds of loads these travelers may have on their backs. You have an opportunity to lighten that load when your day intersects with his/hers. And I'm not talking about his/her checkbook or credit card here. Although that could come into play if we're fortunate!*

Sometimes customers come into our store and show some attitude, and not in a good way. One practice I think is particularly rude is walking into the store with a cell phone conversation going on. Occasionally someone jokes that we should figure out a way to block cell phone reception in the store. Realistically, we wouldn't want to do that. If a customer has a conversation they need to have before settling into shopping mode, it's a smart thing to let them get it over with.

But greeting people in this situation is challenging. There's no easy way once they take off, especially in our larger showrooms. Further, do they want to talk to us or be left alone?

We're in the serving business and we're wise to keep that in mind. Let's face it, we're constantly faced with bad manners. I don't think we want to contribute to that. So it's helpful to remember that the people we encounter may be going through any number of personal crises and issues. Handle them with care.

5. Never stop learning. *Are you green and growing, or ripe and rotting?*

That question was posed to me at a workshop many, many years ago. Recruiters say the most important strength a candidate can possess today is the desire and ability to learn. I don't think this is unique to the present, but it likely has accelerated. I've noticed technology can make smart people who resist it look like dinosaurs. It's unfair, but that's the way it is. You don't have to be cutting-edge, but you don't want to be pulled along kicking and screaming either. I've had people tell me they regret email was ever invented. I remember coming back to a stack of messages and a couple dozen new voicemail messages after being out of the office for a couple of days. I'll take the emails.

I have 100 business-related books in my possession, and I've adapted much of my current thinking from the ideas of smart people. It's worth reading a book, even if you only find one good idea. Then there are books that explain life's important concepts in elegant ways, such as Stephen R. Covey's *The 7 Habits of Highly Effective People*, which I've read multiple times.

There are many other ways to keep learning. Our company belongs to a buying and co-op group, Furniture First. The group consists of over 200 retailers with over 300 store fronts. The organization's goal is helping members grow through merchandising with the use of continuous education and networking. By listening to other retailers and the staff at Furniture First, we've improved our business in many ways. I had the honor to serve on the co-op board, which was a great networking and learning experience.

A few years ago, I took a year-long course, "Leading from Within," through the University of St. Thomas. I recall there were around twelve students, all leaders in a variety of fields—retail, education, engineering, marketing, medical care, home building, and more. The course was taught by a combination of educators. We explored many directions (and I found some uncomfortable), all with the idea of opening our eyes to alternate approaches and reaching a better understanding of our strengths, weaknesses, and passions. Among the many beliefs I firmed up during that time is a good definition of commitment: To say "I'll give it my best" is interest. To say "I'll get it done no matter what" is commitment. I find many people who say they are committed are actually just interested. In one class session, a former prisoner of war in Vietnam talked to us and answered our questions. Talk about commitment. He described how they were tortured until they broke, and as he put it, "We all broke." The former POW told us survival was all about encouragement and helping the next guy. That became his purpose.

In another class session a leader of a jazz band visited. We compared the leadership techniques of a bandleader to what we do. What do you do if you're a bandleader and you have somebody not in tune or who plays a different melody? It's worth thinking about what an employee who similarly isn't able to perform does to the performance of the company.

One of the course instructors, Doug Menikheim, remains a friend and I consider him a mentor to this day. Talk about a life-long learner in service. At over 73 years old, he ran for elected office for the first time and won a position on the Stillwater City Council. He loves it.

I'm always learning, which I think helps us grow as a company and, hopefully, provides a positive example.

6. Meaningful and satisfying work can bring balance to your life. *We've all heard the expression, "Don't bring your problems to work with you." While the intention of this statement may be valid, we all know it's nonsense. Problems are part of who we are as individuals. The only way you can leave your problems at home is to stay at home. It's far better to be aware of your diversions and conduct yourself accordingly. Your work can provide respite from your diversions at times.*

Retail has its demands, there's no question about it. While we try to always think of our customers' needs first, nobody at Schneiderman's would seriously think our work is more important than faith or family. In difficult family situations, we've been supportive and that's as it should be. Almost everyone works because the income provides for them and their families. So if you have to work anyway, why not find meaning from what you're doing? ServiceMaster proclaims as their first corporate objective, "To honor God in all we do." Is it possible to serve God by cleaning a toilet? I honestly think so. Over the years, I've encountered many people who keep searching for meaning when it's right in front of them. Serving others can make us feel happy and worthwhile. I remember hearing somebody put it this way: It is not so much a matter of finding a purpose that gives us joy, as it is a matter of recognizing what our purpose already is . . . and then living it!

I was at a delivery team meeting once and the drivers were discussing a situation with a difficult-to-assemble bed combined with a difficult customer we were trying to satisfy. I was concerned by what I was hearing, but didn't jump in. As the drivers were leaving the meeting, the lead driver who was making this delivery attempt that day put his arm around my shoulder and said, "Don't worry, Larry, we'll take care of your customer." And they did.

We have the opportunity to make somebody's day better. If we do that, the day is not a loss.

7. Every shopper is playing "I've got a secret." *She is at our store because she has a decorating want or need. It takes skill and patience to unlock the secret. This is the crux of effective selling.*

The first person to clue me in about this was my brother Phil. He found it rewarding to earn his customers' trust and have them share information he needed in order to fill their needs. Often people come to the store and tell us they are "just looking." Shockingly, that's not the case. But it doesn't end there. Sometimes, the customer says they're looking for a couch, when in reality, they're thinking about a whole room. A common statement is, "I'm not buying today." Yet once the right furniture is found, the customer goes forward with the order. Or we'll hear, "We have a budget of $2,000." But then considerably more is spent. Sometimes a customer would like to know what the financing options are, but is uneasy about asking. A skillful and caring sales consultant can find the keys to unlock these secrets. A long-time sales educator who worked with us named Peter Marino expressed this sentiment perfectly: "Shoppers often say they are looking for furniture, when in truth, they're looking for a salesperson."

8. Here's something that shouldn't be a secret: Let the shopper see that you love what you do. *I love this quote and you know intuitively it is true: "The society that respects incompetent physicians more than competent plumbers will have neither good plumbing nor good medicine." Through your integrity, enthusiasm, and competence, you bring honor to what you do.*

My dad worked for 21 years in a nail mill. Throughout my life, he would mention his work there. He made it obvious to me that he appreciated, even liked, the difficult work.

In the world of retail—from service stations to department stores—it appears as though a lot of people don't like what they are doing. You know the symptoms. They do the minimum work for you and a smile seems out of the question. You can ask for anything out of the norm and your request is greeted with a quick "no," rather than trying to figure something out. Have you ever asked these folks why they are so unhappy? I have. Most are shocked by the question. Typically, the response will be one of three: 1) no response, 2) they'll claim they're having a bad day, or 3) they'll say they like their job. Well, if they enjoy their job, then why not show it?

In some cases, people in retail are often victims of rudeness themselves. You get what you give, not that it's right. A sales consultant doing their job well ought to be respected. They have strengths and abilities that are being used to mutual advantage. The same can be said for any position. More than ever, people are skeptical of those in what once were the most trusted professions—clergy, medicine, law. Perhaps that's healthy. Regardless, we should all remember that it's not what you do, but how you do it.

It's been my privilege to see excellence in many of our employees over the years, never more than now. Each year we award the President's Award to an employee who meets the ideal of a Schneiderman's associate. All employees have the opportunity to submit a nomination. These are in turn reviewed by a team of five managers, who then make a recommendation to me. Presenting the award is a highlight of my year. I am aware that, as a rule, the nominees are leaders in our company, even when they quietly lead by example. The first recipient of the award—and deservedly so—was Fran Fields, who served from 1984 to 2010 as our controller and benefits coordinator. In addition to being competent and committed to her work, Fran served our associates as her customers, doing everything within reason to serve their needs.

Not too long ago, we had a meeting with our people at one of our locations and one of the younger employees said assertively and publicly, "I want to say, I love my job at Schneiderman's." After the meeting, as I drove back to my office, it occurred to me that many of our employees have told me this in private, but you don't often hear it said in the presence of one's peers. I'm sure this young lady has no idea how much that meant. No coincidence our customers often make raving comments about her.

We do some extra little things to show our employees we care. We remember them with a modest gift on their birthdays. We recognize and express our thanks on their anniversaries at Schneiderman's. Our company newsletter, *Store-to-Store*, prints some of the many positive comments we receive from our customers. I enjoy sending handwritten notes and leaving people messages on their voicemail thanking them for their good work. These gestures are all part of demonstrating how much I love what I do and how important their work is.

9. Some call it "the close." I call it gathering the evidence and calling for the verdict. *My friends know I'm always up for a good meal. Somebody has an idea to go out and eat. Casual? Fast food? Formal? Steak? Seafood? Once we gain a consensus, I always appreciate the friend who steps out and calls us into action. I want to eat. I don't want to discuss every variable of eating out. So it is with our customers. Once the right item has been found and any objections answered, it's a kindness to help a customer finalize her choice.*

In selling circles, it is a common perception that to be a great sales consultant, you must be a great closer. That is true, but a lot of damage can be caused by prematurely suggesting a customer should buy something. When a sales consultant hasn't asked the right questions to understand the needs and then tries to push the customer into buying something he or she doesn't need, that action is likely to remove any trust. In this case, the sales consultant confirms the worst thoughts people have about pushy salespeople. It damages the store's reputation and it reflects poorly on the vocation.

It is far better to view the process step by step—offer suggestions, answer objections honestly, and then only when you feel the customer is in agreement, ask for the sales order. Paul Zimmerman, our long-time sales and operations manager, has noticed that we get far more complaints from customers who felt we weren't helpful enough, rather than we were pushy. It's worth remembering customers want to find solutions and they need our help.

We will sometimes have a sales consultant voice the opinion that they think customers should be left to browse. Not surprising, this approach will not make you a sales leader. When we hear this mentality surface, we drag out our "tire store" comparison. Imagine you need to buy a set of tires for your car. Upon entering, you're greeted by a pleasant salesperson, who says, "Go ahead and browse around at our tires." Okay, now what? Wouldn't it be far more helpful and effective if the salesperson asked some questions like: What kind of car are these for? What happened with the tires you have now? What is your main concern? Is it safety? Is it price? How many do you need?

Some question the parallel with a tire store, but I don't. If anything, a mistake buying tires will be less costly than a misstep with a quality furniture purchase.

A disadvantage of the big furniture stores, including ours, is that it's easy to lose a customer in the showroom. We've sponsored focus groups and we've asked the question, "What is the ideal sales consultant?" The comparison that has often come up is that the sales consultant should be like a great server in a good restaurant, out of sight until you need them. That's easy to say, not so easy to execute. Not too long ago, I visited El Dorado Furniture in Miami and was impressed to notice that their salespeople are required to not only stay available to customers, but to escort them out the door—every time. While I waited for a cab to pick me up, I counted customers leaving and every single one of them was with a salesperson as they left.

One of the more common things customers sometimes say as they're browsing the showroom is, "I'll know it when I see it." I have pondered how a shopper will know it when they see it when, in reality, they don't really know what they need. One of our top sales consultants told me how he works on this "secret." He listens to what the customer says and then asks permission to show them an item. If it doesn't fill the customer's need, he asks, "What should be changed to make this work?" Then they work on it from there. Often the customer leaves happy, having found what she had in mind. I told you he is one of our best.

10. Treat the name of the company you work with as if it's your own name. *Now you may think this is self-serving on my part and to some extent, it is. After all, if our sales associates are successful it benefits Schneiderman's. However, I recommend this strongly wherever and whomever you may work for. Consumers like to work with the owners of a company. Why is that? It's because they think (perhaps sometimes erroneously) an owner will care the most. By showing the shopper you have "ownership," she will see you have a commitment to do the right thing for her and you are likely to be there to serve her in the future.*

Sure, this is a self-serving tenet for someone whose business literally bears his name. And it's natural for any owner to want the people on payroll to respect the company they work with.

One of the important subtleties to me is when our employees talk about a matter concerning Schneiderman's. I love to hear "our" about the store. Conversely, it bothers me to hear "they do this, they do that" about the company.

While we have many employees who are long term, we do have a number of positions that tend to not be career jobs. Still, life moves by quickly and even if a person is going to be here for only a couple of years, it's in everyone's interest to make that a good couple of years. It's rewarding to be part of something successful. I know this is easy for me to say, even self-serving, but nobody should work for a company if the values of the company don't match the employee's values. Over the years, I've had employees come to me a few times and tell me they didn't feel something was right or fair. We take things like that seriously. I can't expect an employee to treat us with respect if there's a perception the company doesn't respect the employee. What about people who are not team players or people who live life with a chip on their shoulder? It's a tough call. I can think of a couple of people in our company who radiate negativity but in reality, they do their jobs well. Often, these personality types tend to be hiring mistakes. It's unlikely we can change somebody who has a dim view of life. In cases where people do their job well, but are negative, managers need to weigh the positive and the negative. If the plan is to live with it, reminders are necessary and care must be taken that these employees work in non-public roles. Do we give up? No.

11. Mistakes. We all make them. *When you make a mistake, be bold! Take ownership, make things right, and vow to yourself not to make the same mistake again. It may be necessary to repeat these steps. Here's where you can be glad we are in the furniture business and it's unlikely that an error on your part will be fatal.*

Here's where I reveal that one of the beautiful parts of being an owner is that I can bury my mistakes in most cases, and I've made some big mistakes. But guess what? My employees seem to appreciate that I'm willing to admit making mistakes. I feel strongly that we should all learn from them. Sometimes that's the only positive outcome of a mistake. This is another example of the importance of good management. If a manager has shown the proper attitude toward employees making mistakes, they are much more likely to be told by the employee (rather than a dissatisfied customer) when a mistake has happened. This can save a great deal on customer satisfaction and management time. When an associate makes a mistake and feels bad about it, encouragement is called for. Never kick a person when they're down.

While all of us are in "customer care," we have people who specialize in this area. Sometimes, we drop the ball. In the words of our long-time services manager, Mark Berg, sometimes things happen that are not our "shining moments." The first thing we need to say is, "I am sorry."

I hope never to hear, "Sorry about that," in one of our stores. That expression sounds like you're not sorry at all.

12. "Retail is detail."—Sam Walton. *Who can argue with Sam Walton, founder of Wal-Mart? Not me. It is helpful to remember why we need to get the details right. One little error in entering a number can ruin a customer experience. Knowing this, we look for possible concerns that may evolve over the sales process and we pay attention to details right down to going over the sales order closely with our customer. We do this because we care about his/her experience with us.*

I'm a detail guy. Being detail oriented can often be accompanied by a love of minutia. I have to watch that. There's an old saying that goes something like this: "A penny saved is a penny earned—but it's still only a penny!"

We dealt with a Canadian vendor who was extremely difficult for us to work with. We had some credits coming from them and they just would not pay us for what we felt we were due. The amount was significant to us and two other capable associates got to the point where they had no leverage to go further with their requests. Enter Larry, the owner. I had the ability to tell them we were willing to part ways with them if they wouldn't live up to their commitments. After more negotiation, the national sales manager told me, "Larry, you are relentless." I thanked him for the compliment.

A tremendous number of behind-the-scenes details are critical to both customer satisfaction and our profitability. There are people in our company every bit as detail oriented as I am. In fact, our northern general manager, Rob Lattanzio, has a paperweight on his desk that I gave to him in thanks. It reads "Rob Lattanzio, Relentless Jr." Sometimes, I call Rob "Junior" when he makes a nice catch. Every so often, he calls me "Senior" under the same circumstances. Some people have this strength, others may not.

This can be a challenge with sales consultants. Customers are unaware of all the details we must get right from the time their order gets into the computer to the time it's delivered. They hopefully will remain unaware. Such won't be the case if a sales consultant enters nearly anything wrong on their order. One wrong digit can result in a red sofa instead of a beige sofa. There are many more examples. The ongoing challenge is that many of our sales consultants are creative right-brain, rather than detail right-brain. So, we have devised systems to try to catch these things at the onset. Similarly, while we have the best technology for receiving furniture at our distribution center, a mistake in receiving can again result in issues with our customers.

Another important area where "detail" is important is visual display. We take a lot of pride in putting together rooms in the store that are not only good, but exciting and idea-provoking. Housekeeping is so important in how the customer views our store. Price tags must be correct in every way and even hung uniformly on the furniture. This is something small to the customer, but also something that makes a big difference. I never tire of seeing fresh, new settings by our talented display team, Susan, Natalie, Chad, Cyndee, Stephanie, and Megan.

There are so many little things that make all the difference in a customer's experience. When our delivery schedulers call our customers, they always confirm the address and the items we intend to bring. This little procedure prevents some serious customer dissatisfaction when customers respond with statements like, "That's my old address," or "What about the mattress I added to the order?"

13. The Law of the Farm. *I will finish with this because I truly believe it's irrefutable. I may have repeated this analogy a bit more than was deemed necessary by my children. But nothing worthwhile in this life occurs without care. The Law of the Farm means planting, watering, fertilizing, and tending daily. Without work, only weeds grow. Learn every day. Prune what doesn't work. Repeat what does. Don't take anything for granted. Follow up. Follow up again. It's more work this way, but you'll feel joy when you see the results!*

No doubt, my strong belief in this law comes from watching my parents develop their business a step at a time. And, like good farmers, they loved their business and were not tempted to do things the easy way. They had their opinions of what was the "right" way and that is what they did.

While it is a generality to say nothing good in life comes easily, I think it's an accurate description of life in the business world. A great read on this subject is *Built to Last* by James C. Collins and Jerry I. Porras. Long-term businesses need solid foundations and then they need to hire capable people one at a time. Yes, as on the farm, sometimes weeds grow and if you're not diligent, the weeds can overpower the crop.

There is no point at which you can put down your proverbial hoe and let the business take care of itself. Things change; you have to master the basics, but be open to improvements.

There is satisfaction in being a part of success that may not have come easily, but came by doing a lot of things right.

These are all lessons I've learned from siblings, friends, coworkers, customers, and frequently from my parents. Schneiderman's has changed as much as any business does over seven decades. In good times and bad, we grew—constantly learning. Would I do things the exact same way as my father? No, of course not. I knew that even as a teenager, when I first had dreams of running the store. As my dad reminded me once as a young man, he might have gotten me where I was, but it was up to me to keep myself there. Dad was a true entrepreneur, even a gambler. The risks Russ and I took were more calculated. Dad wasn't fond of "managing" the business. I've enjoyed the challenges management presents.

My Dad's Way, and My Way

When I talk about my dad in today's world, it may sound like he was rude. It was so different back then. There were so many things he did, or said, that I wouldn't even consider. For example, my dad hated to sell carpeting. Selling carpeting could be tedious, and really, the customer was dependent on the salesperson for help. Added to that, a lot of it looks alike. So, it's time-consuming. People often bring in diagrams and all these samples that look alike. My mother would be the first to get a carpet customer. If she were busy with another customer, then I would get the carpet customer. Eventually my wife, Sheila, started working at Schneiderman's and she was good at selling carpeting. Well, one Sunday we had three customers and they were all interested in carpet. So, here we all are in this small, confined carpet area. We are all showing samples. This one guy says to my dad in a loud voice, obviously wanting the other customers to hear it, "I can buy this same carpet for $2 a yard less at Goldfine's."

My dad looked at him, took a $20 bill out of his wallet, laid it on the table, and said, "I'll bet you that you can't find that carpet for $2 a yard less at Goldfine's."

The guy said, "I don't want to bet."

Dad puts another $20 down on the table and said, "I bet you can't find this carpet for $1 a yard less at Goldfine's."

The guy said again, "I don't want to bet."

So Dad puts another $20 down, and he said, "I tell you what. I think you and I both know you won't buy any carpeting from me today. I'll bet you $100," he says as he puts two more twenties down, "that you can't buy this carpet for the same price at Goldfine's as you can buy it here."

The guy said, "I don't have $100."

"Then you don't have any goddamn business looking at carpet." Dad made this bold statement while he was scooping up his five twenties, and the couple took off.

Dad, Mom, and I would often visit about the day on Sunday nights as we closed. That night, my dad asked me, "You were embarrassed by that, weren't you?"

I said I was. "I think it was inappropriate."

My mother stuck up for him. She was always a balanced and honest person. Her support could go either way, depending on how she saw a situation. In this case, she felt the guy was trying to create problems and she said to me, "I sold to my customer and you sold to your customer because I think it made the point."

My dad obviously wouldn't have wanted to see *me* do that, but with him, there were certain things that were going to set him off. Dad didn't see gray in many situations; I do. Dad wasn't one to wonder what another person's point of view was. It was his way. He had a strong code of what was right and what was wrong and that's how he operated.

At Schneiderman's today, we often hire people who have little sales experience. They appear to have the aptitude for it, but they don't really know whether or not they're going to like it—or whether or not they'll do well. They have a lot of preconceived notions about selling. If you look at the story above with my father, that was his way of teaching me. He would never have wanted to see me do something like that. In fact, if he had, I imagine I would have seen him hitch up his pants in silent warning, no matter my age. But was he wrong? It took my mom to show me the truth behind the lesson my dad was teaching me, and that he was trying to teach the customer. I would never agree with the approach he took. I would never allow a sales consultant to act that way to a customer. But Dad had knowledge of people and knowledge of selling.

I've also reached a point where I'm passing along what I've learned and expectations I hold for myself and my sales consultants. Many of the 13 lessons I include in the booklet *Simple Little Things I've Learned* are the result of working with people like Clyde Morse. Straightforward, caring, nurturing, truthful—the basics.

Doing It the Schneiderman Way

Early on, we carried a high-quality manufacturer called Hickory, which unfortunately is no longer in business. They had an expensive but beautiful dining set called Bocage. One day there were some folks in the store who owned a pharmacy in Hibbing, Minnesota. This couple was considered quite wealthy. Since I was familiar with all our catalogs, I showed them this set and I was telling my mother how reasonable the Bocage is in price. She said it's beautiful and she liked it, but she didn't know how reasonable it was.

"Well, gee, the whole table and six chairs, for that price?" And I told her how much it was.

"Well, that's not right," she said. So we went and looked. I had taken 35 percent off, thinking I was looking at the suggested retail price. But I had taken 35 percent off wholesale—so our cost, minus 35 percent, and no consideration of freight. I had screwed up badly.

I told Mom they were just thinking about it, so we'd just have to hope they don't buy it. And guess what? They came by the next Sunday prepared to buy it. They had shopped around so they knew the furniture should cost much more money. My mom said she'd take care of it. She told them, "Larry does a great job, but he's only 16 years old. He made an honest mistake. We can't afford to sell it to you for that price. It is the wrong price." She figured out what the price was supposed to be and they weren't happy, but they bought it anyway.

This taught me one of the most important management principles I value. Managers should never walk by a problem and pretend not to see it. My mom saw I had made a mistake, but she didn't let me handle the situation alone. The principle is the same whether you find an employee in a difficult situation or a showroom that should be cleaned up.

Greeting a customer creates an important first impression, and as the cliché goes, you only get one chance for a positive first impression. When someone walks into one of our stores, they need to feel as if they are welcomed. Once I was in one of our stores and I walked by one of our sales stations. The sales consultant standing there didn't even look up. I asked, "Hey, how are you doing today?"

"Oh, it's you. How are you?" she asked.

"Well, you know," I replied. "It could have been worse. I could have been a customer."

Any person who comes in the store deserves a smile and a hello. We should make that person's day a little better, even if we have to work hard to be approachable.

I learned an important lesson from my father right after I started working full time. I had seen a contemporary line called Craft. I liked it. I wanted to buy it, but I knew even then that it would be a stretch for us to buy and sell. My dad absolutely hated it. Actually, he hated contemporary in general, but this furniture was more modern than anything else we carried. I went ahead and ordered it anyway without telling him. I didn't have the guts to tell him. Days turned into weeks and then months. Finally, the Craft furniture showed up and my dad still didn't know. I put it all out and displayed it as best as I could. I flirted with the idea of claiming, "I thought you knew I was ordering this." Finally, he came and looked at it. He took his glasses off and I knew this wouldn't be good. He said, "I can't believe you did that."

"Well, it's sharp and we have nothing like it. I don't think older people will want it, but we are going to get younger people in the store too."

"Nobody's going to like this crap. You're going to be stuck with this. This is going to cost us a lot of money. I'm not going to say anything more about it, but every time you walk by this stuff, just remember what you did."

Crap. It turned out he was right. It didn't sell at all. The only reason we got rid of it all was a leak in the roof that caused a lot of it to get water damage. I may have thought I knew better than my dad did, but he had more experience. He knew what the customer wanted. I did think this furniture was great, but it didn't sell for us. It was an important lesson: Know your customer.

I'd like to say I only made the mistake of not knowing my customer that one time, but I do have one more example that has stuck with me all these years. We had a bricklayer living in the community named Leo Kivela. I liked Leo. He had a camper trailer he would pull behind his pickup to job sites and he needed a mattress for it. My assumption was that he wouldn't want an expensive mattress for this purpose. So I started showing him mattresses and saying to him, "Here's a good mattress for the money." I was showing him a less expensive mattress, but he went to lay down on what was called the Palatial at that time, an expensive mattress. He said, "This is fine, this is nice."

"Leo, that's the best one. It's a great mattress, but it's expensive."

"Larry, it's hard to put a dollar figure on a good night's sleep." I felt guilty as I wrote up the mattress.

It's a bad idea to judge peoples' desire or ability to pay based on appearance, or preconceived notion of what they will spend.

12

The Distribution Center

We do a great job in our distribution and delivery part of our business. Time and again, on the response cards we give to our customers, even when they are unhappy with their experience, which can sometimes happen, they'll acknowledge our delivery team was excellent. We do a lot of things right when it comes to delivery.

We have a bonus system for the drivers. To earn it, the delivery team must have at least 95 percent successful deliveries, and no damage. They must also be within the planned delivery-time window 95 percent of the time. The teams succeed or fail together.

A customer called me one afternoon and asked, "You the owner?"

"Yes," I admitted, feeling cautious. Calls that start like this often are not happy ones.

"Well, I have to tell you. I got a call from your delivery people and they said their truck had broken down and they were going to be late." Oh great.

"Guess what?" she said. "I was pretty shocked when I looked out my window. A wrecker showed up pulling your truck. Your guys insisted on doing the delivery of my furniture before pulling the truck away."

That's a pretty amazing service story.

One reason I'm so proud of our delivery and service is that we went through a period when we were growing in sales, but we had many problems in this area.

In 1998, our metro-area business had become 85 percent of our overall business, and was growing impressively, but our service IQ was not keeping up. We were transforming too many customers into ex-customers. We didn't have people equipped to solve customer problems. Russ and I talked about it almost daily. He was frustrated and he said, "Our business is in the Cities, you should be here."

He was right; it was time for a change. After the move, I was spending more time at the warehouse, and I was immediately appalled about many things I saw. One incident made a particularly strong impression.

It was mid-morning and I received a call from a customer who had some issues with her purchase and our upholstery tech had made some corrections. She looked at it, and sent it back again. She was calling to tell me how unhappy she was with the repairs we made.

"I'm sorry," I told her. "Why don't I take your name and phone number. I'll research this and call you back in an hour, is that ok?"

She agreed and I went and talked to our warehouse manager at the time. "Larry, every so often you run into a customer who you're never going to be good enough for," he told me. "I suggest you give her money back."

I struggle with that philosophy because it doesn't solve any problems. I asked my dad once when I was a kid if he ever thought about giving someone their money back and telling them don't come back to the store. He laughed and said, "I'd never do that because I think it would feel so good, I'd start doing it a lot." I adopted that idea. To this day, I can count on one hand the number of customers I've ever given up on that way. Giving their money back doesn't solve their furniture needs.

When I called the customer back she said, "Okay, so you're going to give me my money back, that's fine. But would you do me a favor, Mr. Schneiderman?"

"Absolutely," I said.

"Did you go look at the sofa and love seat?" she asked.

"No, I didn't."

"Would you go look at it?" she asked. "Look at the skirts on it in particular. Look at the sewing on the arm of the sofa. Then, if you wouldn't mind, call me back, after you look at the furniture. I want you to tell me if your wife would accept it."

I now had a squeamish feeling because she was too reasonable, too nice. I went back out there and said to my warehouse manager, "I want to take a look at the sofa and loveseat. Have the guys get it down. I'll meet you there with the upholstery tech." I'd already determined I didn't like the upholstery tech; my previous interactions with him had made that clear. He was a real know-it-all about everything.

I looked over the sofa and loveseat after they'd taken them down. They looked terrible! The skirts on the sofa were different heights.

The customer had complained about the stripe on the back not quite being straight. So rather than doing it right, the upholstery tech stretched it along the back so now it had a big curve in it. The re-sewn arm seam was an awful job—I mean, just terrible. I looked at it, and I remember how angry I was, and I asked the tech, "This is your best work?"

"Well, I didn't say this was my best work."

"But it was good enough for you, wasn't it?" There was no point in getting a response from him. I said to the manager, "I'll talk to you later. But I'm telling both of you. If you ever embarrass our company again like this with a customer it will be the end right there."

I went and called the customer back immediately and said, "I want to apologize. Quite frankly, the information I was given was that your specifications were higher than we could meet, but after seeing what was done . . ." I was so frustrated I couldn't even finish the sentence. "You asked me if my wife would accept it? No way! I am extremely sorry and we will send you the refund. I'm very sorry."

"I tell you what. I'll make a deal with you. You can reorder the sofa and love seat for me and you don't have to send me a refund if you promise me you will personally look at them before they're delivered again." So that's what I did, and she was happy with the second order.

It was clear that things had deteriorated in our distribution center (DC). It was exasperating. We had a basic computer system at the time, but we were moving to put everything on expensive, more sophisticated software. I had heard from other retailers that the time during computer conversions was the worst in their business careers. We were having severe problems with a number of people in our DC and our DC manager had no solutions, only complaints. The manager responsible for implementing the new computer system and the DC manager were knocking heads daily. I didn't know what I was going to do. I knew our DC manager was the wrong person for the job.

Then out of the clear blue sky one day my receptionist told me someone wanted to see me. I asked for a bit more information. These spontaneous visits can break into your day. She said he was interested in interviewing for a job. I agreed. It wasn't the normal procedure, but that's okay, we're not the U.S. Army.

The man sat down and said his family has a furniture business in Oklahoma, but his wife is from Le Sueur, Minnesota, and they wanted to make a change in their life. "I don't know why, but I was drawn to coming over here. My strength is distribution centers and I'm looking for a management position. Even if you don't have something, maybe you know someone who's hiring. I've heard Schneiderman's is a long-established business."

After two or three more meetings, I could tell that if he could deliver on his principles, he was the person I wanted to manage the DC. I parted ways with the manager we already had, and by then the upholstery tech was already gone. Roger Smith became the DC manager in February 2000, three weeks after he dropped by to visit with me. He is a principled man and lives his faith, but that is not to say he isn't disciplined as a leader.

When Roger took over, we had an ongoing problem with our drivers not being on time. This, of course, leads to not making the deliveries on time. We made our expectations plain to our delivery drivers and they either changed or left.

Many other changes needed to be made. We had to do what a business with problems has to do, and many people left. It was a difficult, but interesting time for us as a company. We had a full-time employee who did nothing but find lost inventory. He wasn't a good employee, but he became instrumental to the sales people because they didn't trust our inventory systems. They would bypass the system and call this kid. They'd say, "We made a delivery and we didn't bring such and such." Then he'd go through the warehouse. He was a full-time employee only doing that—looking for missing products—our mistakes.

Since we turned things around in the DC, we've had 100 percent inventory integrity for years. Whenever we've been audited by the bank or our accountants, we've been 100 percent at the distribution center. When it comes to our associates there,

Roger and I agree that even if they're with us a short time, we want them to feel we were a good place to work and we care about our team and customers.

When my peer group from our performance group has critiqued our DC, they've often commented that we have a pretty old demographic among our DC employees. There's a lot of experience in the ranks. Our Bill of Rights extends to our associates in the DC. They are respected and appreciated. Even if it's not a long-term employment, we work for good outcomes. A good example is a driver who worked for us for only two years while he attended school for information technology. He did good work as a driver and then left when he graduated. Years later, we advertised for an IT person, and guess what? We hired the same guy for the position. He told me he always had the utmost respect for Schneiderman's.

One of the best business books I've read, *First, Break All the Rules* by Marcus Buckingham and Curt Coffman, is based on extensive Gallup research among workers across the U.S. (My daughter Jodi, the industrial organizational psychologist, and I often disagree on what makes a good business book, but we both admire this one. She values the empirical data from the Gallup polls that led to their conclusions. I value how their conclusions can help Schneiderman's in our ever-evolving efforts to improve.) Buckingham and Coffman report that the Gallup research indicates that employees feel about the companies they work for the same way they feel about their managers.

For example, if Schneiderman's has a manager who doesn't treat his or her staff with respect, those people will feel the company itself does not treat its employees with respect. The quality and commitment of our managers critical. I can't emphasize that enough. When I embraced this somewhat startling truth, I became more aware of exactly how dependent we are on our managers. The associates on their teams will actually feel about Schneiderman's the way they feel toward their manager. By extension, the way our associates feel about the company determines how they treat our customers. In this way, the managers stand at the very core of whether we succeed or fail.

There is a saying that goes, "Excellence happens when people care more than is reasonable." I'm often amazed at how much some of our DC employees care about things. A lot of that comes from the direction of Roger, our DC manager. Perhaps the associates in the DC respect him for what he does and how he does it. He will make the tough decisions and he understands how to take care of customers.

One management principle I know to be true is: You get what you reward. We went through a period of time when we were having frequent damage to customers' homes. Inexperienced delivery crews were blamed for this unfortunate situation—and there was some basis for that. My own thought at the time was that we were not properly coaching driving teams. We set up a reward system where we tracked the number of homes each delivery person was in and set plateaus at which each employee would get bonuses based on zero home damage. I enjoyed presenting a nice check to our first driver who tracked 3,000 home delivery stops with no damage. So, at the meeting, I asked him to share his secrets of success with our other delivery people. Though a quiet person by nature, he looked up and said firmly, "Just give a shit." It made an impression on the more recent hires in the room. In any part of our business, "just caring" will go a long way. Several people kiddingly suggested we turn his comment into a new tagline, but I demurred.

Not only do we have great people at our DC, but also in the customer care and administration center (AC). The furniture business has some nuances that can make it a challenge to meet customer expectations. Often, it's not a business where you can just take something out of a box and bring it to the customer.

People don't allow for the fact that furniture is essentially hand-made. Freight damage is another issue. We have a person at our DC whose primary job is to inspect every dining table to make sure the leaves fit and then pack it before it's delivered or picked up. You wouldn't guess this would be necessary—but if he didn't do that, we'd have to exchange a lot of dining tables. That would mean a lot of customer dissatisfaction.

Despite our best efforts, a lot of issues surface in the furniture business. We make up to a hundred stops or more on some delivery days—that's a lot of handling. It's also common for customers to have different expectations than the manufacturers. For instance, a customer purchases a solid wood table and their kids do some writing on the table and some of the lines show on the tabletop. This is not a flaw or a defect, but did the sales consultant specifically tell them this might happen? Some styles of furniture are made to have a "casual," non-tailored look. The more a sofa of this style is used, the more "casual" it will look. Again, this is not a defect, but what if our customer doesn't like it?

Our customer services manager, Mark Berg, performs what may be the toughest job in the company, and that includes mine. We want every customer to be happy with us, but that is just not possible. I once had a customer get upset with me because I couldn't agree with what she was demanding. "Apparently your parents never taught you that the customer is always right," she said.

"My parents taught me that *nobody* is always right," I replied.

Mark and his team operate under the loose guideline, "We will do everything reasonable to satisfy every customer." Of course, "reasonable" is the rub, since it's subjective. We're often called upon to work with customers on issues well past the manufacturer's warranty or where the problem is self-inflicted. We hate to say no and we'll try to figure out something. Yet sometimes, we need to say to our customer, "In order to be fair to everybody . . ." This isn't always a popular statement.

Mark once told me that the people in service wear a wristband that says "WWLD"—*What Would Larry Do?* Of course this puts a smile on my face, knowing the last thing I would want to do is dissatisfy a customer.

I'm happy that over 97 percent of our customers tell us they're pleased with us. Most folks are reasonable and fair. Still, we deal with some hard-to-please people, the "stretch customers." My feeling is, if we are geared up to satisfy stretch customers, typical customers will also be served better.

Mark Berg, June Morse, Kurt Johnson, and the service and delivery scheduling team do important work for us and they treat it that way. From time to time, even today, I will get a call from a disappointed customer. I will always listen. If they've talked to Mark Berg, though, I'm going to feel confident we did everything reasonable. Still, sometimes we drop the ball, and it's important to listen and be open to what a disappointed customer has to say.

13

The Sales Floor

It's a big deal to me that people choose to come to Schneiderman's because there are many other stores they could go to instead. We don't want to disappoint them. I want my sales consultants to feel the same way. If we don't give people in our stores great service, then eventually nobody will have a job.

If a customer knows even the most basic things about sales, then they know if the sales consultant is doing a good job or not. The first thing a customer might notice is if he or she was greeted on arrival. Our stores can be large, and so much furniture can be a little overwhelming for some people. It's important for us to have sales consultants greeting people as soon as they enter our store. The second thing a customer may wonder is often a result of number one: How does a sales consultant address a frequent comment from customers? We often hear, "I'm just looking." How does a sales consultant respond? One of the best responses I've ever heard a sales consultant say was, "That's great, we love people looking at Schneiderman's. Are you looking for a mattress or furniture?" From those two starting points, customers may already know 70 percent of what they need to know about wanting to work with that sales consultant. This is a big deal, not only for us as a company, but also for the sales consultant in a commission-based pay system.

We used mystery shoppers for a while, but we thought it caused more problems than it solved. This led our operations manager of 24 years, Paul Zimmerman, and me to take the stance that using mystery shoppers is something we probably didn't want to do again. One thing we have to keep in mind is mystery shoppers take time away from commission sales people. In the sales consultant's mind, they could have been waiting on another customer. This isn't fair to either the sales consultant or the actual customer waiting for assistance. Nonetheless, six months after we stopped using mystery shoppers, some of the sales people were saying, "I'm pretty sure I had a mystery shopper last night." The sales staff was becoming paranoid their customers were mystery shoppers, and that tension doesn't help build trust. There is a place for mystery shoppers, but we haven't used them since the early 2000s and I don't know that there is a place for them in a commission sales area. If we did employ mystery shoppers again, we would compensate the staff for each good report.

We can't have a manager on duty all the time, so doing things right is left to our sales consultants most of the time. And often when a manager is on duty, he isn't out on the floor, but busy doing administrative things instead. One of the practices at retail stores that annoys customers is when salespeople chat among themselves in a customer's presence. One good furniture retailer put it this way: "De-cluster and get customer-ready." I notice this cluster phenomenon often when I shop at different stores. Just as annoying is the salesperson who hangs around the customer even though they aren't wanted and aren't adding to the experience. We like to say, "If you're not helping, you're hovering." Sure, we would like every customer who shops at our stores to buy from us. We know that's not possible, but even when a customer isn't buying, we still should make our best effort to help make it a pleasing experience. It's good business to do so because the customer who doesn't buy today will likely be interested in furniture later.

So what happens in the evenings and on Sundays when the manager isn't there? Sales consultants have a lot of extra time and there are things they could be doing, but some don't do them. One of our practices is that every customer is supposed to get a post-delivery phone call. If the consultant's customer got a sofa, then she calls the customer to make sure he's happy. If a sales consultant has decided "sales won't be my career, won't be my work," they tend to take shortcuts. They don't make phone calls or send thank-you notes. The people who do well follow through on these things. In that way, success is self-fulfilling. For example, every salesperson receives an "open order report" that they can print off daily. At a minimum, they should print it off once a week. This report shows all the orders they have entered into our ordering system that haven't been delivered yet. They are supposed to review those orders and if the promise date is soon, the sales consultants had better know the status of the order before the customer calls. It is always better for us to inform the customer when an order is expected to arrive, or is going to be delayed, rather than the customer calling us to ask where their order is. The sales consultant can simply call and find out what is going on with the order, then call the customer to report, "I've been assured your order is going to be in on such-and-such a date." We go over those things all the time, but some people don't do them, at least, not consistently.

We have a number of sales consultants who write the good numbers. One of the things they often do is schedule design visits at the customer's home. We have people who have design degrees, which are helpful, but what we try to foster is a less intimidating experience with a salesperson house call. They will make an appointment, go to a potential customer's home, take pictures, make a diagram, and then meet them back at the store with some recommendations. We will also give customers recommendations for paint, drapes, and carpet even though we don't sell those. Often, the consumers are reluctant for a couple of reasons. One, people most often want to feel as if they made the decision on their purchase without assistance. It is their home and they don't want to feel as if they have been pressured into buying something they eventually will realize they don't like. Another hesitation is that they might feel they have an obligation to buy something, i.e., someone comes to my house and so now I have to buy. Sometimes they think we're going to start talking renovation, knock this wall out, do this and that. It's not that way, but it's what some think. The impressive thing about a good sales consultant is they schedule their house calls on their day off. Most people wouldn't do that. But the top performers are committed and goal oriented. They are talented, and have great follow-through.

Of course, there are some nuances. Not all the sales consultants are full-time. The great majority are, but the position is also a terrific opportunity for part-timers, if they work weekends. I'd say our part-time sales consultants are making between $20 to $40 an hour. But they are around when the store is busy.

Mastering the Website

One of the biggest changes over the years has been the growing importance of the Internet and our website. It's a fact that over 85 percent of women shop our website before they shop our store. We've done some research on how well we do and we stand up really well. Different philosophies can be seen by reviewing furniture websites. Some of our competitors don't list their prices, at least at the time of this writing. The theory often used to justify this practice says that it's a good thing to encourage the customer to call, thus furthering the relationship. Perhaps, or do shoppers just look for a site with the prices? Intuitively, if I am looking at wristwatches, what good is it to see all these wristwatches if I don't know the price?

Another thing many of our competitors do to make customers think they have a lot of merchandise is show furniture on their website that they don't actually stock, but they can get. It's not like they are being dishonest. We don't stock it, it's not in our showroom, but we can get it. That's no longer our website policy. In our case, this was another lesson learned. We had people unhappy when they would come to our store after seeing a product on our website and we didn't have what they were looking for. Our sales people responded with clear feedback: Only put the stuff on the website that we have. And that's what we did. There likely isn't one site that's best for all customers, but we've done some wide research and we rate well with women 35 to 62, which is our most important demographic. Website management takes a tremendous amount of time. We have one person dedicated to the website full-time who works in conjunction with my son. It's not at all unusual for Jason to call me late in the evening and excitedly ask me to go online and check some new feature.

In many cases, the consumer thinks that if you don't show a product on your website, you don't have it. This isn't the case for Schneiderman's. Many items we carry aren't on the website. We should try to show everything on our website that we have in our store. We might make it too easy for people, but our philosophy is to make the buying process painless and transparent. We have the manufacturer listed right alongside the items on our site and I don't think other stores do that. Our understanding, informed by 65 years in business, is that people want to compare. The downside is that by having the prices on the site, people can get price comparisons across the country. A wildly low price isn't always what it appears. Consider the apt maxim: When you buy quality, you only cry once. It's easy to find a low price for furniture; copycats of popular styles abound. We encourage shoppers to consider how they'll handle a problem with an item, should one crop up. No store has the lowest price every time. A solid reputation for service is often the tie-breaker in a customer's choice of a retailer.

We're told that currently about 12 percent of all furniture is sold over the Internet. I think that when people care about their furniture, and how it looks and feels in their home, you can't improve on a good sales consultant in a good store with good furniture. However, if somebody wants to buy a sofa and not *the* sofa, an Internet purchase is an alternative to consider. Personally, it amazes me that people purchase sofas and chairs, furniture they'll likely live with for some number of years, without making sure they're comfortable and the quality is something they'll be happy with.

We monitor our phone calls for quality control purposes. And we actually do listen to a sampling of calls. The recorded calls are shared with the appropriate manager and sometimes me. One recent call particularly caught our interest. A woman calling asked about a $3,000 leather sectional on our website. "Do you have it in stock?" she asked.

"Yes," our sales consultant told her. "There are three in stock."

The customer decided to place the order. Our sales consultant, trying to do the right thing, agreed to write it up, but suggested she come in and sit on the couch. The caller responded crisply, "I don't have that kind of time."

We delivered the sectional a couple of days later. We hope they're happy with it.

14

The Remarkable 2012

Despite the concerns of much of the past few years, 2012 had some remarkable highlights. With consumer confidence up and down, and the deaths of my brothers Phil on July 30, 2010, and Russ in 2011, I couldn't help but feel somewhat overwhelmed personally and professionally. I needed 2012. Schneiderman's enjoyed a nice sales increase that year. My youngest daughter, Jenna, married. My mother celebrated her 100th birthday. And we hosted the Russ Schneiderman Memorial Golf Tournament.

It's not as if we are a charity-driven company, but we have had the good fortune to be able to contribute to the community and we search for new ways to do more. For example, we had the privilege to donate 40 rooms of furniture to Habitat for Humanity on our 40th anniversary in 1988. We believed this was a meaningful way to reciprocate the loyalty that many Minnesotans have shown over the previous 40 years. We committed to supplying a living room, dining room, or bedroom set to the next 40 homes built in Minnesota by Habitat for Humanity.

It was a great success and the first major donation of furniture Habitat for Humanity ever received.

Russ and I attended the open house for the first recipient family. She was so appreciative of her new living room furniture. She told us she'd never been in a home with new furniture. I thought she meant she had never had new furniture, but told us she meant nobody she knows has new furniture. Russ and I reflected on that comment afterward; it was another reminder of how fortunate we've been.

Schneiderman's also works with an outstanding organization called Bridging. When a customer buys a piece of furniture from us, we offer to pick up their used piece if it's in good condition. We then have that item delivered to Bridging, which is an amazing operation that cleans everything and then provides a shopping experience for families in transition at their locations in Bloomington and Roseville. Utmost attention is given to the family's dignity. We have recycled over 12,000 pieces of furniture through this program.

So we have been involved with our communities through various charities, but our efforts with the Ronald McDonald House have been the most important.

As of 2013, we have contributed over $450,000 to the Ronald McDonald House, largely through an annual golf tournament and auction. Our relationship with the Ronald McDonald House evolved from my brother Russell's son, Joey, who at age five died of lymphoblastic leukemia on May 20, 1988. During his illness, Russ and his wife, Monica, spent a year at the Ronald McDonald House and became believers in their mission. In 2011, there was no golf tournament because Russ was ill and he and Monica had carried the weight of organizing the event since its inception in 1990. So it was with great pride on June 28, 2012, that Monica, their daughter Molly, and I led an amazing group of volunteers in our first Russ Schneiderman Memorial Golf Tournament.

Many people contributed to the success of the tournament and auction, but one of my favorite moments involved a young artist named Christine Tulgren. When I received her email, I was a little surprised.

Christine's message said she was a painter—an abstract painter—and she wanted to paint something for the auction. We met shortly after, and Christine told me about the moment she knew she wanted to be involved in the Ronald McDonald House. As Christine tells her story:

> I was standing in line at the University of Minnesota [Hospital] talking to a woman and her daughter. "Yeah, we're so excited because today is Lydia's last day," the woman said, referring to her daughter.
>
> I said, "Last day, what do you mean?"
>
> "We've been here for two months. My daughter has a brain tumor, cancer, and she's going under radiation and chemotherapy. She went blind because of it. We've been here for two months and today she gets to go home."
>
> I couldn't imagine living through something like that. The little girl is positive and the mom is positive.
>
> The mom said, "If it wasn't for the Ronald McDonald House I don't know what we would have done because they provided us a home and we didn't have to worry about food or laundry, or anything. All of our family could be together and we didn't have to go through this alone."
>
> I told Larry that story and he looked at me and said, "Can you speak at the fundraiser?"

"By chance or by faith, I met this little girl and her mom," is how Christine started, and then she continued with her story. She concluded, "I'll leave you with this. Helping families starts with one." She was in tears when she finished.

When Monica went to bid on Christine's painting, someone else beat her to it. Back and forth the bidding moved. I looked over at Christine and as the bidding grew and grew, I could see she couldn't hold back the tears. I can't imagine what it must have meant to her. The final bid was substantially beyond what anybody expected. Monica was the winning bidder, and she then donated the painting to the Ronald McDonald House. I was happy for Christine.

Russ had always wanted to have 144 golfers for the tournament. In 2012, we reached that goal for the first time. In 2013, we did it again. The tournament honors Russ's memory and his mission to support Ronald McDonald House. It has been truly a great success in every way.

After the Russ Schneiderman Memorial Tournament, 2012 ended with another high note: Mom's 100th birthday on December 18, 2012. She was a modest person, who wasn't thinking much about turning 100. She told us not to plan anything big. How could we not, though? The family planned her 100th birthday celebration at our Duluth store. I was pleased with the turnout. As I've worked on this book, I've had the opportunity to look back on Mom's journals and listen to old audio files of her and my dad talking. It's hard to believe how much she accomplished, and the number of years we were blessed to have her near us. I can't think of anyone I've admired more in terms of strength, resilience, kindness, and faith. I am more like her than my father in some ways. Perhaps that's how she was able to teach me patience, understanding, and the foundation of my moral beliefs—all things I consider the core of who I am. Once some years ago, a Meadowlands pastor I'd just met told me he'd asked a couple of his parishioners who knew my family what I was like. He told me they'd said, "You'll like Larry. He's a lot like his mother." While not deserved, that's the best compliment I've ever received.

15

Parkinson's Disease and Passing the Torch

I was at the High Point Furniture Market in April 2011 when my daughter-in-law, Natalie, asked, "Have you ever noticed you don't swing your left arm?"

I hadn't noticed before she said something. During the rest of our time at the market, we had a little fun with it. She would push my arm and I would consciously try to swing it. I did start to notice I wasn't swinging it unless I did it intentionally. Later, I Googled "limp left arm." The good news was it could mean a lot of things. The bad news was it could mean Parkinson's disease. I was hoping for the former. For many years, I've served as a Befriender through our church, a ministry that serves shut-ins. My first two Befriended folks both died from complications of Parkinson's disease. So I had seen it close up.

In March 2011, my wife and I were visiting friends in Florida. Our friend Parin Winter is an internist and she commented to Sheila, "I think Larry might have Parkinson's disease." She had been observing me. My wife asked her to not say anything to me because in two weeks, I was going to go on a trip to South Africa to visit Jodi and Chris, accompanied by Jenna and Molly. I was really looking forward to it. Sheila was afraid that if I went to be diagnosed, I wouldn't go, and she was probably right. We made an appointment with a neurologist for when I got back.

After the trip, we went to the neurologist who said he was pretty sure I have Parkinson's disease, but I didn't know for sure. So I went to a Parkinson's specialist, who informed me that there's no test to diagnose Parkinson's disease. It's all observational. She said the most common symptom is that you don't blink. When I mention not blinking, I start to think about it, and then I blink. But when I'm not thinking about it, my eyes get dry. Another common symptom that I have is a slower gait. Gait is one of the most affected motor characteristics of the disorder. I am by no means to the point of shuffling while I walk, but the slowness is there. My brother Russ commented a couple years ago when he saw me get out of the car, "You get out of the car like you're 90." He was joking, but it was an astute observation. I guess I hadn't realized it so much, but Russ was right. Like my arm not swinging, and loss of the ability to smell, I start to pay more attention to new symptoms.

The specialist was just about positive, but felt I should get a second opinion, since it's pretty important to know.

Growing up in that little town of Meadowlands, typical class sizes were 20 to 30 people. In the class two years below me, Russ's class, there was a kid by the name of Jerry Vitek. When Jerry was in junior high school, he began to share with everyone his ambition to be a doctor, and from then on, he never swayed from this goal. While Jerry's parents, Gladys and Frank, have passed away, I remember them well. Frank worked in the mines for a time, and later did maintenance work for the county. Gladys brought in $1.25 per hour working for the phone company. Frank worked on cars at night to make additional income. Sometimes we would go over to their home in Meadowlands, and I think I'm pretty safe when I say Gladys was one of the nicest people I've ever known.

When Jerry graduated from college, he applied to medical school. In fact, he applied to 11 medical schools. For his efforts, he received 11 rejection letters. He took a position as a teaching assistant while in graduate school to try to reduce the financial burden on his parents. Meanwhile, he continued to apply to at least 11 medical schools every year, receiving rejection letters in every case. Others in the same situation would have given up, but the rejections only made Jerry more determined. After years of rejection, an interviewer at the Mayo Clinic asked, "What will you do if you don't get into medical school?"

Jerry replied, "I will apply again."

The interviewer looked at him. "No, you don't understand. What I mean is, what will you do if you don't get into medical school?"

To which Jerry replied, "No. *You* don't understand. I will apply again."

Jerry didn't think the interviewer believed him and figured he'd get tired of applying, or more likely would not reapply. It wasn't in him to give up, and he never did.

Jerry did get into medical school and earned induction into Alpha Omega Alpha, the medical students' honor society. Along with other neuroscientists, he became a pioneer in the treatment of Parkinson's disease through deep brain stimulation (DBS). When performed in those earlier years, the operation could take up to 12 hours and was done while the patient was awake so he or she can respond as metal probes are carefully inserted deep into the brain. It's fascinating, and Jerry has appeared on national television broadcasts and in magazines for his part in the success of the treatment. Not bad for a kid from Meadowlands,

Minnesota.

I decided Jerry should be my second opinion. I contacted a mutual friend in Duluth and he gave me Jerry's contact information. At the time, he had just left a position as co-chair of the Center for Neurological Restoration at the Cleveland Clinic, a top medical facility. I reached Jerry and he said the timing was good—he'd just moved to St. Paul to begin a new position as chair of the Neurology Department at the University of Minnesota. "Why don't you and Sheila come over to my office in the research building and we can spend some time together?"

The three of us talked for a while, shared information about our mutual acquaintances back in Meadowlands, and then he had me walking and doing a number of different movements. He observed the no blinking and said, "Larry, there is no doubt you have Parkinson's disease and it's progressed more than I would have pictured. You've likely had it for two or three years." He made a point to be very direct, and concluded with three options. "Larry, I could do any of three things. I could get you a referral to the Mayo Clinic—they are excellent, of course. Second, there is a physician I could recommend here at the University of Minnesota. Or, if you would be comfortable with it, I would gladly be your doctor." Well, this made for an easy choice.

Everybody with a serious health problem would like to have a physician who is regarded as cutting edge. But to be treated by a man I respect highly in every way and consider a friend is nothing short of a special blessing. As Sheila and I said goodbye at the elevator, Jerry added, "Larry, we'll get that left arm swinging in no time. You'll do well. Your faith and positive attitude will make a difference."

Now I knew for sure. I have Parkinson's disease. Even though the two other physicians had suspected that I had it, I was still holding out hope. Sheila and I had a long conversation about it when we got home. The next morning, I read a devotional passage by Dr. Charles Stanley. I suppose almost any scripture would have spoken to me that particular morning, but as it turned out, the reading was based on the passage from 1 Samuel, the familiar story of David and Goliath. It's always been amazing to me how a person can read the same story from the Bible many, many times and with a different frame of mind, understand it in a new way. What I read and felt that morning was that Goliath never had a chance. David, a skilled sling-shot artist, with faith and confidence, was destined to win that battle. After all, in addition to the stone that felled Goliath, he had picked up five smooth stones. Had he missed the first time, David had a backup plan. Parkinson's disease may be my Goliath, but I have my own smooth stones for this battle. Faith, family, Dr. Vitek and his staff, friends, and past experiences all make a difference.

The diagnosis was made in July 2011. I didn't want people to know of my condition at the time, because my brother Russ was ill. I didn't want to divert attention and make a big deal out of things. At that point, only my immediate family knew, and I also shared the news with Russ and Monica. I remember vividly, there Russ was, in so much pain, and in such a bad spot in his life, and yet he was like, "Ohh nooo." It made an impression on me that despite his physical condition he had that kind of compassion, because obviously this wasn't as bad as what he was going through.

I remember when his doctor called him to tell him his cancer had spread to his glands. He and I were eating lunch at a local restaurant when he answered his phone, listened for a moment, and responded, "Well, that's not what I wanted to hear." I was heartsick and couldn't stop thinking about how Sheila and I had been with Russ so long ago when the hospital called and gave him the terrible news that their son had leukemia.

As is so often the case with cancer treatment, Russ experienced highs and lows as the medical providers tried different approaches with chemotherapy and radiation. One morning—August 19, 2010—Russ came by my office and tossed me a baseball. He had worked at the Twins game the night before. He had a big smile on his face as he announced, "I'm cancer free!" What great news it was at the time. When he left my office, I wrote that date on the baseball: 8-19-10. But soon enough the cancer came back in an overpowering way. The bravery shown by Monica, Molly, and John was steadfast. Russ knew he was loved and despite terrible pain, unrelenting sickness, and discomfort, he told me, "I'm not ready to say goodbye."

Almost exactly one year from that day he gave me the ball, on August 10, 2011, Russ died in the hospital of melanoma. He was a big part of so much of my life. I think about him every day.

After Russ passed away, I shared the news about the Parkinson's diagnosis with my extended family and friends. Then I met with the Schneiderman's managers to confirm the news with them. They were aware that Jason had been taking on some of my responsibilities, but I wanted them to know I had no intention of leaving the business.

I don't think people know much about Parkinson's disease, especially younger people. When you get older, it seems like everyone knows somebody who has it. I think there's often some denial about the symptoms. I don't show the disease much at this point, and the medication seems to be working for now. My goal has always been, and it remains, to enjoy and make the most of every day. I have to plan ahead like anybody else, but I don't spend time worrying about 10, or 20, or 30 years from now. I think my kids have picked up that attitude from me. Sheila has had rheumatoid arthritis since she was in her mid-twenties. The picture she always had about our late life was me taking care of her, so both of us having rather serious health issues kind of changes her confidence.

One treatment theory is that exercise to exhaustion can help the brain produce dopamine, which is what Parkinson's sufferers lack. So my friend Jeff Winter, a certified trainer, pushed me to take up strength training and spinning (cycling). As Dr. Vitek told me, "If the spinning and the strength training turn out not to help the Parkinson's directly, what's the down side?" I'm convinced it has helped, though. If you ever want to view commitment up close, take some spinning classes. I've been active most of my life, but nothing I've ever done wears me out like an hour on those bikes. I have been the beneficiary of some good advice and help.

My family and friends have shown so much support and empathy. Our pastor recently shared with the congregation that he has early-onset Parkinson's disease. As I went to shake his hand after worship, he hugged me and whispered, "We'll walk this journey together." I can't imagine better company.

I think my son, Jason, is probably the least accepting of the situation. Yet he has stepped up to take on additional responsibilities in the company. Jason simply wouldn't talk to me at all about the Parkinson's when I first brought it up. I encouraged him to go to the Michael J. Fox Foundation website, but he wasn't doing it. So one morning we were supposed to have a meeting at 10:00 and I lied to him and said 9:00 so we'd have the chance to talk privately. Before he arrived, I printed off a well-written information sheet called "Somebody You Love Has Parkinson's Disease." I gave it to him and asked him to sit down and read it. Jason shook his head and didn't say anything.

It's time for the second generation of Schneiderman's operating the family business to pass on the torch. I have strong faith and know God has given my family and me a wonderful life. We have received many blessings, and have been able to give back to the community. At the time of this writing, I know I still have many good years ahead of me. I'm approaching the same period my parents faced 30-plus years ago, when Russ and I purchased the business. For Schneiderman's to continue to be successful, it needs strong leadership. I am fortunate to have a son with the passion and drive to continue the business. Jason has already taken on important roles in the company and is adding his own personal touches.

One recent example of Jason's leadership is the renovation of our Woodbury location, which had started to exhibit the inevitable wear and tear buildings eventually show. Jason and I knew we needed a complete renovation, inside and outside. We wanted to expand the store, but the maximum overall footprint of the building allowed by code meant an addition of only 10,000 square feet. Mike Diem, the architect, suggested we explore raising the roof and adding a second floor. We did just that—raising the roof 19 feet. The store needed to be closed from August 1, 2013, through April 5, 2014, but the results are phenomenal.

Jason is a remarkable man. Growing up with a learning disability can be frustrating, tough on self-confidence, and demoralizing. He had a tough time in school for sure. Sometimes Sheila and I wondered if there was anything we could do to turn him around. Fortunately, an exceptional teacher, Jim Ohman, taught us an important lesson. As prophetic as any statement I've ever heard, he predicted Jason's future: "I've had a lot of boys like Jason over the years and here's what I'm going to tell you. I'm going to be blunt. He's never going to do well in school, but he's going to be great in life. He's going to be fine when he's, say, about 22." At this moment as I recall Jason's growth from childhood to adulthood, I can't help but be amazed by everything he has accomplished.

I think people are destined for things in ways we don't always understand. I looked at an article recently that reported on a study by Julie Logan that determined that among the general population, 10 to 15 percent of people are estimated to have dyslexia and/or ADHD. Among the successful entrepreneur population, however, that increases measurably to 35 percent. Dyslexic entrepreneurs reported underachievement at school. And successful dyslexics develop ways of controlling, coping, and compensating for their deficits.

We all have obstacles in life, and while my biggest obstacle is yet to come, Jason has been breaking down the walls in his path since childhood to become an excellent leader. While I have no doubt about the success of Schneiderman's under Jason's leadership, I can't help but feel an even greater sense of pride when I imagine that perhaps he was destined, as I think I was three decades ago, to improve on the legacy left for us by my parents. And I am excited to see how the next phase of Schneiderman's unfolds.

ACKNOWLEDGMENTS

We often hear interesting, even inspiring, stories of business owners who rise from poverty and become wildly successful. These remarkable people are often described as self-made. Those kinds of stories have a wide appeal; they certainly resonate with me, since my dad's journey has a lot in common with those kinds of success stories.

But I've always had trouble with the "self-made" idea. Nobody can be successful in business or in life without the help of others.

I've been the beneficiary of a special mom and a special dad. Who *I* am, for better and for worse, reflects the proverbial apple falling not too far from the tree. Dare I suggest that any person who has had the benefit of loving parents is given a head start in life that not everyone is blessed to receive? So I would first like to thank my parents. I have spoken of them often in this book, but they have provided so much over the years that I can never hope to document it all. My dad was prophetic when he told me, "Larry, you'll sell more furniture than I ever sold, but you'll never make the money I did." He was right. We did well continuing their legacy, but all of it follows behind the determined labor of my parents. They were the ones who fashioned the business principles we still use today, built the Schneiderman's brand, fostered customer devotion, and crafted the foundation for what we have become.

Though I have many blessings, I can honestly say I am most blessed by my family. I am thankful for my children—they are a great joy in my life. Jason and Natalie, Jodi and Chris, Jenna and Collin, I cannot express how much I love you all. My siblings, David, Karen, Phil, Claudia, and Russ, have been important individuals in my life, as have their spouses Bob, Michael, and Monica. I especially want to express my thankfulness for my 35-year partnership with Russ. We worked well together, achieved goals together, and liked each other along the way. We succeeded as business partners, friends—and as brothers. I have so many other family members who have had a positive influence on me—nephews, nieces, uncles, aunts, cousins, and more. Thank you all.

Friendships have enriched my life so much. You know who you are! Thank you for the fun, the understanding, and the companionship.

You will notice the byline of this book says, "With Jody Mabry." Thank you, Jody, for all your help. It's been a pleasure getting to know you. It was about two years ago now that you told me, "Larry, we will write and rewrite as many times as you want." I've appreciated your willingness to do whatever it takes. Thanks for the interest you've shown toward my family and the business. And thanks for the nice furniture order!

While I'm at it, I was the recipient of excellent help from the people of Beaver's Pond Press. I appreciated their enthusiasm, support, and professionalism.

The true legacy of Schneiderman's Furniture has always been the people who serve our *customers*, directly and indirectly. There can be no success without people who care. Over the years our customers have been served by our many committed associates. So many excellent people have been part of our company, too many to mention in this book. I hope our employees know that a day has not gone by in which my parents, Jason, and myself haven't appreciated all they do to support the company and help it grow. You have our ongoing thanks.

I've asked at store meetings, "What is our greatest asset?" Frequently, the most common response is Schneiderman's employees. While employees play a key part of our business, our greatest asset is our customers. Time and again, I hear about customers who have had a great experience beautifying their homes with our furniture. It is the devotion of repeat customers alongside new customers' first purchases that continues make Schneiderman's successful and unique. If you are a Schneiderman's customer, bless you!

And, saving the most important for last . . .

On September 26, 2013, Sheila and I celebrated our 43rd wedding anniversary. We reminisced about our wedding—the wedding we needed to hold in the evening, after the store closed. The men in the wedding were almost late because Russ, Phil, Clyde, and I needed to unload the furniture from a Flexsteel truck that arrived just as we were leaving for the church. I'll never forget the driver commenting that we were the best-dressed unloaders he had ever seen. That's right, we unloaded the truck in our tuxedos.

From the start of our marriage, Sheila understood and supported me in my work. After we were married, Sheila asked, "I know you need to work weekends, but what day will you have off so we can be together and do household things?" I told her that if I needed a day off, I could take it. She held firm and insisted I talk to Dad about taking at least one day a week off. That was a new concept for both him and me. So, I went to my dad and told him that *Sheila* wanted me to take one day off every week, and we thought Wednesday would work. Dad gave me a confused look and said, "Well, if you need a day off, take it off." I held out for every Wednesday, and despite his agreement, I could feel the ground shaking under his feet. Then he asked,

"What labor union are you joining?"

So Sheila and I were ready for our first Wednesday off together, but I still needed to measure a customer's house for carpet, and check out a complaint for a different customer. I guess it's hard to break old habits. Needless to say, Sheila wasn't too happy with me. It wasn't quite the day off my 21-year-old bride had in mind.

I recall another unfortunate Wednesday when I was measuring another home for carpeting while Sheila stayed outside in the car to read. In the company of the very conversational customers, I forgot she was out there. When it occurred to me that Sheila was in the car, I told them I needed to go and why. I can still remember the look on the customer's face, as if he was wondering what kind of a nut case I was to leave my wife waiting outside for so long. I'll admit, forgetting about her didn't make for the most pleasant day. In time, though, I started enjoying our day off and only called on customers if it was truly necessary.

It's difficult for me to imagine life without Sheila. She has shown so much support all of these years, while I have expended a large portion of my time and energy into the furniture business. I'm profoundly thankful to her for insisting that I be a decent husband and a pretty good dad. Before smartphones, I emulated my dad by carrying a small spiral notebook virtually at all times. When an issue or thought came up, I automatically wrote it down so I wouldn't forget it. Sheila knew nothing recorded in that little book would be overlooked, so if one of the kids had something going on, she would write something like: "Jodi's Christmas program at the school, Dec. 20th, 2 p.m." And I never missed any of the events she jotted down in my notebook.

Nothing is more important than raising children, and ours have been true blessings. Jason sometimes will joke—at least I hope he's joking—that I was never home when he was a kid.

There is, I suppose, some truth to that. Also, when I was at home, my mind was distracted by business concerns. Sheila's perseverance helped me understand the urgency of being present with our family—and what a gift that was. According to an old saying, "You can only be as happy as your unhappiest child." Well, Jason, Jodi, and Jenna are ethical, positive, and fun people, and they married well. I can't imagine what could be more important, and I know Sheila played a central role in preparing them to lead satisfying, productive lives.

From our first date—a homecoming football game when she was 15 and I was 16—through the triumphs and struggles that have marked our lives, to whatever the future holds, I'm profoundly grateful to be making this journey with Sheila next to me.